Studies in
Writing & Rhetoric

IN 1980, THE CONFERENCE ON COLLEGE COMPOSITION AND COM-munication perceived a need for providing publishing opportunities for monographs that were too lengthy for publication in its journal and too short for the typical publication of scholarly books by The National Council of Teachers of English. A series called Studies in Writing and Rhetoric was conceived, and a Publication Committee established.

Monographs to be considered for publication may be speculative, theoretical, historical, or analytical studies; research reports; or other works contributing to a better understanding of writing, in-cluding interdisciplinary studies or studies in disciplines related to composing. The SWR series will exclude textbooks, unrevised dis-sertations, book-length manuscripts, course syllabi, lesson plans, and collections of previously published material.

Any teacher-writer interested in submitting a work for publica-tion in this series should send either a prospectus and sample manu-script or a full manuscript to the Senior Editor for Publications, NCTE, 1111 Kenyon Road, Urbana, IL 61801. Accompanied by sample manuscript, a prospectus should contain a rationale, a defi-nition of readership within the CCCC constituency, comparison with related publications, an annotated table of contents, an esti-mate of length in double-spaced 8½ x 11 sheets, and the date by which full manuscript can be expected. Manuscripts should be in the range of 100 to 170 typed manuscript pages.

The works that have been published in this series serve as models for future SWR monographs.

Dialogue, Dialectic, and Conversation
A Social Perspective on the Function of Writing

Gregory Clark

WITH A FOREWORD BY ROBERT J. CONNORS

Published for the Conference on College
Composition and Communication

SOUTHERN ILLINOIS UNIVERSITY PRESS
Carbondale and Edwardsville

Production of works in this series has been partly funded by the
Conference on College Composition and Communication of the National
Council of Teachers of English

Printed in the United States of America
Edited by Susan Thornton
Designed by Design for Publishing, Inc., Bob Nance
Production supervised by Linda Jorgensen-Buhman

Library of Congress Cataloging-in-Publication Data

Clark, Gregory, 1950–
    Dialogue, dialectic, and conversation : a social perspective on
the function of writing / Gregory Clark : with a foreword by Robert J.
Connors.
        p.   cm. — (Studies in writing & rhetoric)
    "Published for the Conference on College Composition and
Communication."
    Bibliography: p.
    1. Dialogue.   2. Authorship—Social aspects.   3. Reader response
criticism.   I. Conference on College Composition and Communication
(U.S.)   II. Title.   III. Series.
PN1551.C54   1990
808′.0014—dc20   89-6214
ISBN 0-8093-1579-3   CIP

93   92   91   90   4   3   2   1

To Ruth, Elayne, and Linda

Contents

Foreword

Robert J. Connors

REVOLUTIONS IN COMPOSITION STUDIES ARE A DIME A DOZEN. Thomas Kuhn did us no favors when he proffered that seductive analogy of the scientific revolution. Now we've overused the term so badly that it has been worn smooth as a prewar nickel. The student-centered revolution. The process revolution. The back-to-basics revolution. The rhetorical revolution. The revolutionary textbook. This revolutionary drillbook. This revolutionary red pen. . . .

To each her own revolution, I guess. But something's been brewing out there, drifting into consciousness from a footnote in a book you'd not read, heard down the hall as a sort of half-understood conversation, found carefully delineated, no doubt, in some thirty-page article in one of those smaller journals that are a little too specialized, a little too theoretical, a little too weird. . . . No, I don't get that one. I wish our library did. Parlorsocialversationdialogiclecticconstructionist. Not quite made out, not quite getting through. Out there, though, definitely out there, a buzz at the edge of consciousness.

But then one night, in one of those free-for-all crowdfests where college comp types go for free food and booze at CCCC—maybe the Harcourt party that Friday night, where they ran out of the little sandwiches early and you had to stand by the table cutting gouda for half an hour to get something to go with the Budweiser that was the only beer they were serving—and looked out through the Bud buzz at the faces in the semidarkness standing and talking and you realized that *this was it*. This bunch of people was the whole situation, the sine qua non, that without which nothing you had been trying to say—or BE—for years and years now would have any meaning. These minds, these scotch-dulled, wine-wild heads out of which any idea of you comes and into which all ideas of you go; these mouths chewing on crackers and grapes and always on the words words words (that are, after all, the only things we have to keep us from the dark); these hands that had inscribed on your own brain all the words you'd ever need, all the words you could ever use; these eyes scanning the black-on-white lines from which you constitute any self outside the buzzing of blood, the immediacy of talk, or the warm shock of skin across skin. . . .

For a long time—who knows what metaphysical dream we were living?—we had been scratching around with fragments, isolated elements, sequestered theories, disconnected atoms. Assumption: you can learn about something by taking it to pieces. Assumption: putting pieces together makes a whole. Assumption: the Self creates significance. Assumption: numbering and ordering systems create self-evident, objective meanings. Assumption: the writer is an Artist, alone, supreme. . . . Come into the lab and we'll tell you about things as they really are, really must be because we can really prove it. I've come out of the garret to tell you things about your own garret because my garret is very well known.

Who was it, whose the "first voice" to say that you couldn't try to do it all in the lab anymore? That the writer is never alone in the garret? Wrong question. As if in very proof of the idea itself, the voices all seemed to swell like the chorus of a Bach motet up together. It was as if we woke up one day in Atlanta in the cool spring of 1987 and we all knew the words to the music. And of course it was a song that we could then see had been sounding in our ears since Gorgias built that solid-gold statue of himself at Delphi, each ounce of gold given by someone melted into communion by words.

Dialogue, Dialectic, Conversation. Words in the atmosphere, heard everywhere now. But where do they come from, where can we take them, what can they make us? Greg Clark is looking carefully in this book at what those words really mean to us. This book is wonderful in pointing us toward some sources of wisdom that we might have heard of—in passing, meaning guiltily to read some day after this stack of papers is done—and showing how many disparate strands fit together. In philosophy, in ethics, in political thought, this idea of making meaning together through words is being raised.

And it is only right that we in rhetoric, who never really did give up the agora and the forum to the lab and the garret, place ourselves in the middle of this confusing but exhilarating spectacle.

Greg takes us in this book on a quick but extremely useful tour of the Zone that we're trying to learn to live in now. Exhilarating, yes. But scary, very scary. This social constructionist deal doesn't solve too many *problems* for us, does it? It was kinda *comfortable* back in the lab and the garret, no? Kind of warm, nice boundaries to the experiment, nice boundaries to the self? A place for everything, everything in its place. Now instead we're out here where mysterious winds are blowing, where all the stable foundations are in danger of melting like Dali watches. Is nothing provable? Have we no real matrix of selfhood at all? Is reality merely a more or less constant scanning pattern? Is everything we teach just propaganda for our own prejudices? Conflict, consensus, opinion, truth are not just words for us anymore—because suddenly we are nose-to-nose with the great responsibility that has always been ours. This isn't just a theoretically interesting scenario for us. We have to *go out there and do something.*

Because we're writing teachers. We're where the rubber meets the road. Our teaching will either have to reflect these social-construction ideas or not. We can't be neutral because we have to meet those kids tomorrow and look 'em in the eyes and tell them what we think the true names of things are. And then listen to what they say, read what they write. And in doing that, we will either go back to the lab, or back to the garret, or we'll stay out here in the wind, with them, maybe trying to huddle together to keep warm.

Greg Clark is a good guide to this strange place where we now find ourselves. He can take us a long way, but from there we'll have to go on together. Hang on tight.

Acknowledgments

I WOULD LIKE TO THANK THE COLLEGE OF HUMANITIES AT Brigham Young University and my department chair, William A. Wilson, for providing me with time to initiate and complete this project.

I am indebted to S. Michael Halloran, Lee Odell, and Annette Kolodny, with whom I first developed these ideas; to colleagues and students whose responses have helped me clarify them; and, particularly, to Grant Boswell and Kristine Hansen, whose thoughtful readings of the complete manuscript were immensely helpful as I began final revisions.

I am also indebted to the members of the NCTE Publications Committee for Studies in Writing and Rhetoric for their responses and encouragement; to John Bennett and Michael Spooner of NCTE for their support; and to Kenney Withers, Susan H. Wilson, and Susan Thornton at Southern Illinois University Press for their help in bringing this project to smooth completion.

Finally, I am indebted to the women in my life—to my grandmother, Ruth Bright, and my mother, Elayne Clark, who first taught me about community; to my wife, Linda, who gives me hope that we can reconstruct our communities for the better; and to my daughters, Casey, Tessa, and, now, Rebecca, who give me good reason to put that hope into practice.

Introduction

IN *INVENTION AS A SOCIAL ACT* (1987), KAREN BURKE LEFEVRE argues that the writing of a text is an inherently collaborative process, that, in her words, "rhetorical invention . . . is an act initiated by a writer and completed by readers, extending over time through a series of transactions and texts" (1). What this amounts to, LeFevre argues, is that the individual writer and the community of which she is a part are necessarily "coexisting and mutually defining" (35), and it is the purpose of LeFevre's study to describe how writers interact with the communities they address in the process of writing a text. The contrasting but complementary purpose of this study is to describe the larger process within which writers and readers coexist and mutually define themselves, and to do so by examining the shape and the function of that series of textual transactions that is the larger social context within which every text is situated. In other words, I am describing the process through which writers and readers use their ongoing exchange of texts collaboratively to construct their collectivity. Consequently, I emphasize not how writers write texts but how writers and readers collectively use them—how we use the texts we write and read to negotiate what we can together believe, value, and do. Throughout this study I argue that what this collaborative textual exchange perpetuates is the fundamental process through which we constitute many of the communities in which we live and work.

Recent literature in philosophy, cultural anthropology, literary theory, rhetoric, and communication, as well as our own literature in composition studies, has asserted that people define the beliefs and values that guide their individual as well as collective actions through a collaborative exchange they sustain through their discourse and, particularly, their texts. This literature uses three terms to describe this process of discursive exchange that seem, at first glance, interchangeable—*dialogue, dialectic,* and *conversation.* A closer reading, however, suggests that some useful distinctions can be made among them. The term *dialogue* describes the cooperative shape of that process, an exchange of discourse that is characterized by its participants' consciousness of each other, by their conscious efforts to interact cooperatively. The term *dialectic,* by contrast, describes its collaborative function, how that process of exchange enables people to construct together assumptions and agreements they can share. The familiar term *conversation* describes that process itself, the natural experience of cooperative, collaborative interaction through which people enact the essence of compromise. Common conversation seems to have an unregulated life of its own, moving of its own momentum in directions in which, as it proceeds, its participants discover themselves wanting and needing to go. Throughout this literature the term *conversation* is used metaphorically to describe this kind of undetermined, democratic exchange with the shape of dialogue and the function of dialectic that provides its participants with the sense of common progress that we experience when we freely converse.

Our primary project in composition studies is to learn for ourselves and teach to others how writing enables individuals to define and sustain their connections with community. This study is an attempt to contribute to that project by using the metaphor of conversation to synthesize from many of the disciplines we draw upon various descriptions of this fundamental social process of discursive exchange, and to argue that this synthesis can provide us with a perspective on the social function of texts that will show us the common ground on which our most ancient rhetorical treatises and our most recent discourse theory can stand together. By unifying our diverse descriptions of the social function of written discourse, this perspective can help us better understand for ourselves what it is people do when they write and read, an understanding that will help us better teach our students to write and read well.

This conversational perspective on writing designates the exchange of texts as the way people discover and validate the common beliefs and values that allow them to live and work together—the shared knowledge that provides the foundation upon which they construct community. From this perspective, writing does not transmit truth: it allows people to define for themselves truths they can share. As John T. Gage puts it, writing viewed in this way "has knowledge as its goal rather than operates on knowledge as raw material" (154). What this perspective suggests is that social life is essentially a rhetorical process, a sustained discursive exchange through which we collaborate in constructing statements that articulate the agreements that bind us together as cooperating members of a community. Such a rhetorical view of social life was taught by the Sophists of fifth-century Greece, who professed that people who are political equals share responsibility for their community, that as citizens they must use the exchange of discourse to define for themselves a community that meets their common needs (Barrett 13). It was also the view taught by professors of rhetoric in the colleges of the early American republic. Chauncey Allen Goodrich of Yale emphasized this political function of discourse when he declared to the students he was preparing for citizenship that "all our institutions and our government are suspended on the contest of mind going on around us," a contest, he emphasized, that is sustained through rhetorical exchange (ix). This fundamental connection of rhetoric and democracy persists in the minds of most of us who teach composition. We teach writing because we believe it enables people to participate in the self-governing communities—whether public, professional, or personal—where their lives and work are situated. Most of us persist in some form of the belief that, as James A. Berlin puts it, "writing courses prepare students for citizenship in a democracy, for assuming their political responsibilities, whether as leaders or simply as active participants" (*Rhetoric and Reality* 189).

The democratic assumptions that underlie this belief are embodied in the perspective on writing and reading presented by the notion that the meaning-making function of every text is situated in the free and collaborative social context described by conversation. This is not the conversation described by Mortimer J. Adler, that one "Great Conversation" of the "Great Thinkers on universal themes" (Graff 163). That is a conversation we can only witness, one that, as it attempts to impose the authoritative truths a particular tradition would perpetuate, is, in its very constitution, undemocratic. In contrast, there are innumerable versions of the conversation I describe: this undirected interaction of equals who engage in the process of sharing the responsibility for conducting their collective life when they find that individual and collective well-being requires them to coordinate their beliefs, values, and actions with others. In terms of writing, what this notion of conversation provides is a perspective on textuality rather than a method for composing texts. It reminds readers that they must reject the claim to authority inherent in every text they read as it reminds writers that they are in fact collaborating with the readers they address by portraying readers and writers alike as coparticipants in the perpetual process of constructing the common knowledge that will support their collective life.

In the first three chapters of this study I draw upon diverse descriptions of this process of textual exchange to present this unifying perspective on the social function of written discourse. Chapter 1 draws upon notions of dialogue from philosophy and literary theory to describe the cooperative shape of this process. In doing so, this chapter explains the epistemological assumptions that support it—assumptions that treat communication itself as a collaboration that makes meaning that can be collectively held—and examines in detail a theory of texts that demonstrates that dialogical shape. Chapter 2 draws upon notions of dialectic from ancient and modern rhetorical theory to describe the collaborative function of this process, a function that enables writers and readers to construct together particular meanings they can share. I develop this description upon my reading of Plato's *Phaedrus* as a description of a dialectical rhetoric that designates every text a temporary act in an ongoing transaction where knowledge of truth is being constructed, and my reading of Aristotle's *Rhetoric* as an attempt to put that rhetoric into practice through the methodology of the enthymeme. I use the work of contemporary commentators on these classical texts to clarify this notion of a dialectical rhetoric that makes writer and reader equal partners in the process of negotiating knowledge they can share. Chapter 3 draws upon current research in oral communication as well as rhetoric to describe writing and reading in terms of the process of conversation itself, a description that complements the current work in composition studies that situates writing in the collaborative social context of a discourse community. My purpose in this chapter is to present the conversation process as a demonstrative model for the social context in which written texts function, a process of exchange with a dialogical shape and a dialectical func-

tion that enables people to use their texts to define their commonality for themselves.

In the last two chapters I discuss the implications this perspective
on the social function of texts has for our teaching. In Chapter 4, I
argue that the conversational perspective prescribes an ethics for
the use of texts that places primary responsibility for the way a text
functions in a community upon the readers who must respond to it.
It is the nature of a rhetorical statement, particularly one stated in
the seeming immutability of written text, to demand the assent of
those it addresses. Consequently, only those who read that text can
suspend it in the process of critical exchange that sustains constructive conversation. Because the highest value in a collaborating community is to perpetuate that process, we should teach our students
that their first responsibility as readers of a text is to judge that text
critically and respond publicly. Finally, I suggest in Chapter 5 that
when we teach our students that the texts they write and read have
meaning only within the process of critical collaborative exchange
described by conversation, we teach them that their writing and
reading are, indeed, social acts for which they are responsible.
Teaching them to act well when they write and read requires us to
teach them the skill in expression and judgment in response that
together sustain constructive collaboration. We teach that, I argue,
when we teach our students to write and read within this fundamentally rhetorical perspective on the social function of texts, a perspective that designates the texts they write and read as parts of the
public discourse that constitutes the communities that enable them
to survive and thrive.

In all, this study argues that writing and reading are fundamental
acts of citizenship that enable individuals to contribute to the construction of community by making them individually and collectively responsible for it. And because some of the most important
communities we and our students inhabit are constituted through
the exchange of texts, I must finally argue with Derrida that our
individual and collective well-being both demand that "One must
then, in a single gesture, but doubled, read and write."

Dialogue, Dialectic, and Conversation

1

Discourse in Dialogue: The Social Context of Writing

MOST OF US LIVE OUR LIVES IN THE COMPANY OF OTHERS, HAVING learned early that we can meet our most basic needs only with their cooperation. And we have learned that we can cooperate successfully only with others who understand as we do what it is we are trying to do together and how we are trying to do it, a shared understanding we develop through the most basic form of cooperation, communication. In essence, we communicate in an attempt to construct with others the shared sense of common needs and common ways of meeting those needs that will bind us together in what Clifford Geertz calls "a community of agreement" (*Local Knowledge* 177). As we continue to communicate within those communities we are able to continue the cooperative process of working with others to meet our common needs. In communicating we collaborate with others in constructing and continually reconstructing from our commonality the community that enables us, both individually and collectively, to survive and progress, a community comprising people engaged in an ongoing process of renegotiating the beliefs and values—and, consequently, the actions—they can share.

This understanding of the social function of communication is built upon two basic philosophical assumptions that are widely shared in modern thought. The first—that we communicate neither to represent reality nor to transmit it, but to constitute it—suggests that in the process of communication itself we transform our interpretations of experience into the structures of knowledge we use to define for ourselves our reality. What this first assumption asserts is the essential interdependence of language and experience: we can neither put the meaning of our experience into words nor use the meaning of words to signify our experience because words and experience are indistinguishable. As Hans-Georg Gadamer insists, "it is part of experience itself that it seeks and finds words to express it" (377). The second assumption—that we communicate not *to* others but *with* them—suggests that the act of communicating is more a cooperative interaction than an assertion of self. Thus, this assumption asserts the essential interdependence of language and social interaction. The process of using words to make sense of our experience is necessarily a cooperative one because, in Gadamer's terms, "language has its true being only . . . in the exercise of understanding between people" (404). When communication is understood on the basis of these two complementary assumptions it becomes, above all, a collaborative process through which a community of people construct a shared understanding of their common experience that provides the foundation for their continued cooperation.

Although Walter Ong's observation that "to speak you have to address another or others" seems to state the obvious, its implications are far-reaching. We *must* address others when we speak because, in Ong's terms, "to formulate anything I must have another person or other persons already 'in mind.'" That is because every statement we make is necessarily "shaped in its very form and content by anticipated response" and, indeed, "calls for response" (176–77). From this perspective, communication is a process of social interaction constituted of an ongoing exchange of inherently interdependent statements and responses, a process that is frequently described as dialogical.[1] Most current discussions of communication as dialogue have their roots in Martin Buber's paradigmatic study, *Between Man and Man* (1947), which locates our essential humanity in the dialogical act of "one being turning to another as another . . . in order to communicate with it in a sphere which is common to them but reaches out beyond the special sphere of each" (203). Buber calls this common sphere the sphere of "between," where communicating people can transcend their separate "personal existences" (203–4) to find meaning they did not know before in "the unity of the contraries" that they separately represent (Friedman 3).

The dialogue that Buber describes is less a structure or method of communication than a perspective on the process itself, what Richard L. Johannesen describes as an "attitude," or a kind of "stance" (374). This dialogical stance is very different from the stance that most of us are taught to take when we write, one that allows us to objectify the people we address as uninformed beings we must attempt to inform with the truth. Given this stance—Buber calls it the "I-It"—our purpose in communicating is to control others by imposing meaning upon them. Communication driven by this purpose functions, in Buber's terms, as monologue rather than dialogue in what is essentially an attempt by one person to dominate others, or, as Maurice Friedman puts it, to "incorporate the other into [the] self" (89). Buber advocates an alternative, dialogical stance that he calls the "I-Thou," a stance that transforms communicating people into coequal collaborators who cooperate in the process of negotiating meanings they can truly share, meanings that do not embody the dominance of one. The purpose of communication from this perspective is to enable people to develop a shared understanding of their common experience in an interaction that becomes, for Buber, more than the sum of its individual participants because the shared knowledge that emerges from it cannot be reduced to what each one of them separately knows. The fundamental element of dialogue, then—its lowest term—is this act of collaboration, an act that constitutes the "reciprocal bond" between collaborators from which their sharable meaning can emerge (Stewart 188).

The purpose of this chapter is to explore this notion of communication as dialogue by examining further the philosophical assumptions that support it and by explaining a theory of the social function of language that describes it. These two assumptions—that communication is the process of meaning making and that it is a collaborative process in which the meaning that is made is meaning that can be collectively held—express a social constructionist epistemology that defines knowledge as negotiated by the people who are to share it, people bound together by common needs and purposes. Both assumptions are embodied in a theory of dialogue developed by Mikhail Bakhtin during the middle decades of this century, a theory that describes all language and particularly writing as func-

tioning within the social context of a community of people who are
necessarily engaged in the continuing process of constructing shared
knowledge through the interaction of their communication. Bakhtin
provides what is perhaps our most comprehensive discussion of
communication as dialogue, a discussion that examines in particular
the dialogical function of written discourse.[2]

The Social Construction of Knowledge

In an essay that examines the literature of social construction as
it applies to the study of writing and reading, Kenneth Bruffee defines this perspective in terms that root both our knowledge and our
communities in our use of language:

> A social constructionist position . . . assumes that entities we normally
> call reality, knowledge, thought, facts, texts, selves, and so on are con-
> structs generated by communities of like-minded peers. Social construc-
> tion understands reality, knowledge, thought, facts, texts, selves, and
> so on as community-generated and community-maintained linguistic
> entities—or, more broadly speaking, symbolic entities—that define or
> "constitute" the communities that generate them. ("Social Construc-
> tion" 774)

From a social constructionist perspective, then, we communicate
with others who share similar experiences for the purpose of coming
to a common understanding of our circumstances, an understanding
that not only binds us together as a cooperating community but also
provides a foundation for our continued communication. This foundation enables us to revise and extend that understanding as our
shared experience and shared circumstances change. From this perspective, communication is an ongoing social interaction through
which we collaborate with others in the continuous process of reconstructing the common interpretation of the world that enables us to
live and act together.[3]

As Bruffee notes, much of the current literature of social construction is built on the work of three scholars whose separate ex-
aminations of the knowledge that their different disciplines comprise have provided germinal expressions of this perspective on the

nature of knowledge. What Thomas Kuhn, Richard Rorty, and Clifford Geertz each describe is a community of people bound together by particular versions of experience that they share: by assumptions, values, and methods that they have agreed to treat as the specialized knowledge of a discipline. Instead of accurately representing an absolute reality, such knowledge, for all three, expresses current interpretations of pertinent experience that a particular community of people have agreed, for now, to consider true. In light of that definition of knowledge, each scholar encourages his disciplinary community to revise the traditional notion of their common project: Kuhn argues that the proper work of science, Rorty of philosophy, and Geertz of anthropology is less to preserve and transmit a particular body of knowledge than to sustain the collaborative process through which accepted interpretations are continually challenged by new ones that reflect the changing experiences of the people who compose that community. In other words, they argue that the primary project of a discipline should be to perpetuate the process of exchange through which disciplinary knowledge itself is continually reconstructed.

In *The Structure of Scientific Revolutions* (1970), Kuhn refutes the notion that scientific knowledge is an expanding body of empirically verifiable truths by asserting that what we consider scientific knowledge is actually the current interpretation of particular experience that a community of scientists has come to consider persuasive. In essence, knowledge among scientists is, at any given time, what those who are most persuasive in a community of scientists agree that it is. For Kuhn, then, learning science is less a matter of mastering a body of facts than of acquiring fluency in the language that enables participation in the exchange where that persuasion occurs. In other words, people become scientists by learning how to participate in the discourse through which scientific knowledge is continually constructed. "Scientific knowledge," asserts Kuhn, "like language, is intrinsically the common property of a group or else nothing at all" (210).

Rorty describes the work of philosophers similarly, as less a matter of discovering "an antecedent reality that has been waiting to be unearthed by analysis or reflection" than of using a particular language in a process of exchange through which a community of philosophers examines together the validity of a concept of reality. "If there is one thing we have learned about concepts in recent decades," observes Rorty, "it is that to have a concept is to be able to use a word, that to have mastery of concepts is to be able to use a language, and that languages are created rather than discovered" ("Philosophy in America Today" 193–94). In *Philosophy and the Mirror of Nature* (1979), Rorty defines philosophical notions of truth in the same way Kuhn defines the scientific, as socially constructed products of the discourse of a particular community. The traditional project of philosophy, to validate our interpretations of experience on the basis of absolute "foundations of knowledge," is, for Rorty, "simply an automatic and empty compliment which we pay to those beliefs which are successful in helping us do what we want to do" (9–10). Instead, he argues, philosophy is a perpetual process of defining and justifying sharable, usable beliefs, dedicated not to the end of establishing truth, but to enlarging "a linguistic and argumentative repertoire, and thus an imagination" ("Philosophy in America Today" 193).

Geertz describes anthropology in similar terms, but he expands the social constructionist perspective beyond the boundaries of disciplinary knowledge to describe as also socially constructed the kind of general cultural knowledge that gives structure and direction to people's lives. Geertz places the process of social construction at the center of human experience and action, arguing in *Local Knowledge* (1983) that "our consciousness is shaped at least as much by how things supposedly look to others, somewhere else in the lifeline of the world, as by how they look here, where we are, now to us" (9). We all situate ourselves, according to Geertz, within a notion of reality that we have constructed with others from shared interpretations of our relatively narrow common experience. In Geertz's metaphor, we are necessarily suspended in these webs of culture that we have spun for ourselves (*Interpretation of Cultures* 5), an assertion he elaborates by demonstrating that governing structures as fundamental as law and common sense reflect not universal truths but agreements of a particular community. We live, Geertz writes, by "local knowledge; local not just as to place, time, class, and variety of issue, but as to accent—vernacular characterizations of what happens connected to vernacular imaginings of what can" (*Local Knowledge* 215). Ultimately, Geertz argues, with Kuhn and Rorty, that knowledge is what we make it, and his subtext, like theirs, argues that we must take responsibility for that knowledge and, thus, for the perpetual process of remaking it in which we are necessarily engaged.

The process of making knowledge begins when people recognize that they need each other, that they must cooperate. In order to cooperate, they begin to define common interpretations of experience that they can treat as their collective reality, a reality constituted in terms of the shared needs, values, and purposes that are the foundation upon which they can sustain the cooperation that maintains their community. This constructed foundation is what Thomas B. Farrell calls "social knowledge" ("Knowledge, Consensus, and Rhetorical Theory" 5, 12). But Farrell reminds us that this social knowledge has its origins in the particular preferences that individuals articulate as recommendations for collective belief and action. Once affirmed by the assenting response of others within the community, those preferences can function there as definitions of what is essentially "preferable public behavior" (8), and what began as one person's preference becomes what a community of people know. In Farrell's terms, the knowledge that comes to be shared by the members of a community first emerges as a provisional assertion in which the consensus of the community is "attributed, or assumed"; that consensus is "confirmed" when the community enacts it in an affirming response (9). Thus, what we come to consider knowledge emerges from an exchange of discourse—essentially, an exchange of arguments—that has the power to transform individual interpretations into the "public conviction" (11–12) that can function within a community as truth.[4] This is the power of communication for which every individual who participates in that process must share the responsibility.

Rorty is concerned that once people affirm the truth of the social knowledge they have constructed they tend to deny its origins, and his concern reaches well beyond disciplinary communities alone. Once confirmed by consensus, shared interpretations take on the appearance of certainty, a certainty that offers a refuge from the responsibility that is inherent in the process of constructing knowledge. Rorty suggests that every community can preserve not only its awareness of the contingency of social knowledge but also the continuity of the exchange in which that knowledge is continually reconstructed by privileging the kind of discourse that continually challenges what its members think they know. If reaching agreement is the purpose that guides our discourse, Rorty warns, we will tend to constrain that discourse with assumptions that will validate particular beliefs as absolute truth and make fundamental disagreement inconceivable. That is, when agreement is the purpose of an exchange, what Rorty calls "normal discourse"—discourse that embodies accepted assumptions and propels the exchange toward a self-fulfilling end—is the only kind of discourse that is allowed to function as communication within that community. If a consciousness of the temporary and contingent status of socially constructed knowledge is to be preserved, the purpose of an exchange must be not to reach agreement but to sustain the process of exchange itself. Only that purpose will admit discourse that challenges existing assumptions, that keeps provisional agreements open to question and revision. Such "abnormal discourse" raises questions and poses alternatives, disrupting consensus and propelling people toward new ways of understanding their common experience.

From the social constructionist perspective, then, the process of exchange must remain incomplete in order to keep every version of reality open to revision and refutation. As we use language to collaborate in the process of constructing sharable notions of the world, we produce meanings that must be suspended in a balance between their function within our community as knowledge and their provisional status as our constructions. We can preserve this balance only by remaining constantly engaged in the fundamental cooperative process of communication itself, a process that has the shape of a dialogue.

Bakhtin's Theory of Dialogue

Mikhail Bakhtin's (1895–1975) description of the dialogical function of language is becoming increasingly important as we develop not only a better understanding of the social function of written discourse but also the essential interdependency of reading and writing.[5] For people studying rhetoric and composition as well as for those studying literature, Bakhtin's work provides perhaps our most comprehensive explanation of the process through which social knowledge is constructed in a cooperative exchange of texts.[6] However diverse its particular applications, Bakhtin's explanation persistently and explicitly affirms the two complementary assumptions about language that support a social constructionist point of view: that our language creates rather than conveys our reality ("a word is not an expression of inner personality; rather, inner personality is an expressed or inwardly impelled word" [*Marxism and the Philosophy of Language* 153]), and that it does so in a process that is collaborative rather than individual ("language . . . lies on the borderline between oneself and the other . . ." because "the word in language is half someone else's" ["Discourse in the Novel" 293]). But Bakhtin's purpose goes beyond presenting a social constructionist perspective, beyond analyzing and explaining the dialogical process of collaborative meaning making, to arguing that because the language we use makes us, unavoidably, participants in a meaning-making dialogue, we must hold ourselves responsible for that meaning we help to make.

Because he believes that any one person's perception of experience is, by definition, necessarily partial, Bakhtin argues that each person who participates in the process of communication is held answerable for what she communicates to others. This insistence upon each person's essential "answerability" in any communication situation is the thesis that underlies all of his work.[7] Indeed, because the discourse of one must always interact with the discourse of others, any statement must function within the immediate context of a dialogue, where it is exposed to the judgment and response of others who hold the maker of the statement responsible for it. Such answerability, for Bakhtin, is a primary fact of our existence: "Life is dialogical by its very nature. To live means to engage in dialogue, to question, to listen, to answer, to agree, etc." (Todorov 97). Bakhtin's recognition of the inherent answerability of our language and thus the responsibility we carry into our social experience, experience made meaningful through our constant communication, is at the core of his lifelong project: to affirm the ontological and the ethical necessity of treating our communication as participation in a dialogue.

Bakhtin's conviction that communication is a collaborative act and that knowledge, whether individually or collectively held, is a product of that collaboration asserts what is for him the ontological reality of dialogical communication. For Bakhtin, "to be means to communicate" because we are inherently devoid of "internal sovereign territory" and must live situated "always on the boundary" of self and others, necessarily looking "in the eyes of the other or through the eyes of the other" (Todorov 96). Consequently, anything we might communicate is "wholly determined" by our "immediate social experience and the broader social milieu" (*Marxism* 86). Because we can understand our own experience only in terms of its commonality, we are continually confronting each other with a mandate to construct from separate perceptions a common interpretation. If individual experience is organized and made meaningful only when it is expressed in the language of collaboration, then dialogue is the form our communication must necessarily take (*Marxism* 85).

Bakhtin asserts the ethical necessity of dialogue in his insistence that language can never be neutral. People bring to the interaction of communication a set of beliefs and values born of the particular experience, beliefs and values their language cannot help but express: "in actuality, we never say or hear words, we say or hear what is true or false, good or bad, important or unimportant, pleasant or unpleasant, and so on. Words are always filled with content and meaning drawn from behavior or ideology. That is the way we understand words, and we can respond only to words that engage us behaviorally or ideologically" (*Marxism* 70).

Because language used in discourse is, for Bakhtin, inherently ideological, expressing as it must one person's judgment of a particular set of experiences, he, like Buber, must condemn any discourse that is monological, that "denies that there exists outside of it another consciousness, with the same rights and capable of responding on an equal footing, another and equal I." Bakhtin rejects, in other words, any discourse that "pretends to be the last word" (Todorov 318). Instead, he celebrates discourse that acknowledges itself as incomplete, as the partial perception of one, as a statement that joins other incomplete statements expressing diverging ideologies in a dialogue where each is held answerable for itself in the interaction of assertion and response. In this dialogue all statements are exposed to the collaborative process of judgment, revision, and redefinition that enables people to construct beliefs and values they can genuinely share.

He explains his dialogical notion of communication in theoretical terms most concisely in *Marxism and the Philosophy of Language* (1929).[8] Here Bakhtin begins with statements about the basic nature of language that are strikingly similar to the theoretical statements that support much contemporary literary theory: the word is not "a stable and always self-equivalent sign"; it is, instead, "an always changeable and adaptable sign" (68). Further, the expressed "word is a two-sided act . . . determined equally by whose word it is and for whom it is meant" (86). Lacking any determinate meaning, then, language becomes meaningful only in the particular social context that is created when people use it to interact. Bakhtin describes such language-in-context, language made meaningful in a particular social interaction, in his discussion of the "utterance," the basic element of communication in his theory of dialogue.

An utterance embodies one person's interpretation of an experience expressed to another, an interpretation that is at once both descriptive and ideological (Todorov 53). It brings together through interaction the common language and the divergent experiences of particular people who must collaborate in constructing a shared interpretation. Consequently, the meaning of any utterance is not in the words alone but in the concrete situation those words express, a situation created by social interaction at a particular time and place. An utterance develops this meaning in a dialogical process, but one that involves two levels of dialogue that Bakhtin designates *internal* and *external.* Before the utterance of one person can confront another in the external, or interpersonal, dialogue that is situated in their social interaction, the person who will utter it must construct it in an internal, or intrapersonal, dialogue where it emerges both in response to the memory of relevant, related utterances that have preceded it and in anticipation of others that will follow it. From that internal collaboration of utterances remembered and imagined emerges a construction of words that have particular meaning given the combined experiences of the person who expresses them and the person to whom they are addressed. That is why, Bakhtin argues, no utterance is the product of one person alone: "Within the arena of . . . every utterance an intense conflict between one's own and another's word is being fought out. . . . The utterance so conceived is a considerably more complex and dynamic organism than it appears when construed simply as a thing that articulates the intention of the person uttering it" (86).

But an utterance alone does not communicate. For Bakhtin, communication does not occur until the utterance of one person is understood by another and *understanding*, as he uses the term, is not passive—it is a deliberate act. Bakhtin's notion of understanding requires more of those to whom an utterance is addressed than simply recognizing the linguistic forms; it requires knowing what those forms mean in a particular social context (68). What must be understood are the representational and the ideological particulars of the interaction in which the words of an utterance are generated, what Bakhtin calls its "theme," and a theme can be understood only in terms of a "concrete, historical situation" (100). Such understanding is constructed in a second internal, intrapersonal dialogue, this one within the person to whom an utterance is addressed, a dialogue conducted in response to the utterance of another. Understanding an utterance, says Bakhtin, requires one "to orient oneself with respect to it, to find the proper place in the corresponding context," which requires, in turn, that "we . . . lay down a set of our own answering words" (102).

The internal, intrapersonal dialogues within which one person's utterance and another's understanding are constructed, then, are situated within and dependent upon the larger context created by the external, interpersonal dialogue in which the utterance and understanding interact. That means that utterance and understanding are not only dialogical in their origin—they are dialogical in their function as well because, in Bakhtin's words, "understanding is to utterance as one line of dialogue is to the next" (102). Within this interpersonal exchange, utterance functions as a dialogically constrained assertion and understanding as a dialogically constrained response: each must emerge in full interaction with the other. Indeed, any utterance must inevitably express an understanding, and any understanding must inevitably respond to an utterance.

Although the utterance is the basic element of Bakhtin's descriptive theory, an utterance without the response of understanding is inherently incomplete. Consequently, Bakhtin emphasizes that the basic component of communication is the dialogical interaction of utterance and understanding, for each is constructed in terms of the other and they cannot be separated from their interaction in the dialogue, where they function together to construct sharable meaning. Communication, for Bakhtin, is founded upon this primary interaction of utterance and understanding in the dialogue that is generated by the attempt of two people to cooperate. In his words, "the real unit of language that is implemented in speech is not the individual, isolated, monologic utterance, but interaction of at least two utterances—in a word, dialogue" (117).

Writing and Reading as Dialogue

Bakhtin presents his theory of dialogue in *Marxism and the Philosophy of Language* using terms that describe oral speech, but in his work on problems in literary criticism he applies these ideas to written communication. One of the most comprehensive of these applications is his long essay, "Discourse in the Novel" (1935). This essay, like most of Bakhtin's work in literature, focuses on the novel because Bakhtin found represented there the authentic pluralism of language that people actually experience, a pluralism that demonstrates the complex and inevitable interactive exchange of utterance and understanding, what he calls *heteroglossia:*

> The novel is the expression of a Galilean perception of language, one that denies the absolutism of a single and unitary language . . . , that refuses to acknowledge its own language as the sole verbal and semantic center of the ideological world. It is a perception that has been made conscious of the vast plenitude of . . . social languages . . . , all of which are equally relative, reified and limited. (366–77)

In the heteroglossia of actual language use, any word that is spoken or heard, written or read, already "tastes of the context and contexts in which it has lived its socially charged life" (293). The words we can use in any situation, then, are already "populated—overpopulated with the intentions of others" (294). Bakhtin finds words functioning in the novel as they function in life, forming and communicating their meaning in "a dialogically agitated and tension-filled environment of alien words, value-judgments and accents" (276). This is the environment of contingent, context-dependent knowledge and competing ideologies, where every statement is made answerable in the dialogue where shared meaning is made.

Bakhtin values the language of the novel because it simulates the dialogical complexity of actual meaning making. There a theme carried by written words is communicated to a reader only in the actual dialogical interaction of an utterance and an act of understanding, an interaction that, when it occurs in the acts of writing and reading, is not only interpersonal but also intertextual.[9] In "Discourse in the Novel," Bakhtin describes reading as a cycle of interactions through which the shared knowledge of writer and reader develops: in response to an utterance of a writer a reader constructs an understanding. This understanding finds its function as a silent utterance in a dialogue sustained within that reader where she is constructing the meaning of the text. Such utterances in response eventually find their function in the external dialogues of that reader's actual social life. In essence, the reader's utterance in response to the utterance of the writer is itself a text, whether articulated or not, a text that embodies that reader's experience as organized by the writer's language and one that will be expressed, whether in its original form or in some later variation, in an external dialogue that reader will join.

Bakhtin finds in the novel what he finds in the world: language that acknowledges its roots in "a particular historical moment in a socially specific environment," that acknowledges itself as nothing more than products of dialogue, "rejoinder[s]" that express an understanding of other utterances that preceded them (276–77). Like the oral language of conversation, the written language of the novel anticipates the dialogical interaction of utterance and understanding that constitutes the collaboration of writer and reader, not only allowing and inviting but even assuming this dialogue of writer's and reader's texts. Writers of novels recognize that their words will be read in the answering words of the readers that express each reader's own "apperceptive background" (262). That is why Bakhtin finds in the language of the novel a written utterance that is responsible because it does not claim to be complete, an utterance that is itself "directed toward an answer" and, thus, "cannot escape the profound influence of the answering word that it anticipates" (279–80). Whether a particular novel is written in an attempt to address readers as they are or to invoke them as the novelist wishes them to be, the utterances that constitute it must be generated in a dialogue within the novelist in response to prior utterances of others as well as in anticipation of the uttered understandings of readers.[10] In other words, Bakhtin finds in the novel writing that is not only read in the context of the dialogical interaction of reader and writer, but written in that context as well.

This dialogical interaction is, to Bakhtin, the "natural orientation of any living discourse" whether written or spoken because writing that "lives" as authentic communication functions with the interpersonal immediacy of speech in the collaborative context of dialogue (279). Such writing inscribes utterances conceived in the understanding of utterances that precede them; it is composed in the context of the common experience of the writer and those who are to read it. And such writing is subsequently understood in the interaction of the community of people for whom it becomes meaningful. In short, writing that is authentic is, for Bakhtin, writing that engages itself in the process of answerability that is created by dialogue. By leaving itself open to the inherently revisionary understanding of readers, such writing affirms the priority of response. In Bakhtin's words, "primacy belongs to the response, as the activating principle: it creates the ground for understanding, it prepares the ground for an active and engaged understanding. Understanding comes to fruition only in the response. Understanding and response are dialectically merged and mutually condition each other; one is impossible without the other" (282). And although much is written that does not affirm the primacy of response, every text is made authentic in its function when it is read as an utterance that requires the dialogical response of understanding.

The benefits of this perspective on the social function of discourse for one community that constructs its knowledge largely through writing—the community of people who write literary criticism— have been explored by Don H. Bialostosky, who argues that the deliberate practice of Bakhtinian principles would enable that community to construct shared knowledge that is richer and more useful than that they have traditionally shared. Specifically, Bialostosky proposes that those who participate in the exchange of written discourse that sustains that community do so in a way that demands that every text be answerable, a demand inherent in the practice of what he calls "dialogics."[11] If the discourse of literary criticism were to become consciously and intentionally dialogical, Bialostosky argues, the process through which members of that community construct what they know about literature would be opened to alternatives not now conceivable because the current discourse of that community is what Rorty would call "normal": constrained by assumptions that protect current agreements constituting the knowledge that its members share. If people who teach and study literature were to begin writing and reading the kind of discourse that Rorty terms "abnormal," discourse that holds even those assumptions answerable to the revisionary process of dialogical exchange, Bialostosky claims that much would change. First, all the texts that members of that community choose to read, whether primary or critical, would be read dialogically, read in terms of the particular social context in which they were generated, as texts situated "historically or imaginatively in a field of other persons' utterances" (790). Second, all texts written by members of that community would be written dialogically, written both in response to what others have written before and in anticipation of the responses of readers who will hold them answerable. Such discourse would sustain within that community a constant consciousness of where their texts come from, how they come to mean, and how they function there. As the collaborative origin of every text is recognized and acknowledged in that community's discourse, its members would confront the constructed, and thus contingent, nature of their knowledge, and that would enable them to participate more critically in the exchange that maintains it.

Bialostosky's point is that such openly dialogical practices of reading and writing would make that community more deliberate and more responsible in the process of constructing their knowledge. When they read, members of that community would respond dialogically—whether a text is monological or dialogical in its intent—by engaging every text in the active exchange of utterance and understanding within which it becomes answerable for what it presents (790). When they wrote they would write dialogically, producing texts that enact their own answerability by incorporating into that process a consciousness of the larger collaborative process of assertion and response of which it is a part. In essence, Bialostosky argues that a community of scholars and critics who read and wrote dialogically would construct more satisfying and useful versions of knowledge about literature:

> As readers sophisticated by an art of dialogics, then, we would self-consciously represent the voice-ideas of others and involve others in dialogues they had not anticipated, but we would also self-consciously expect unexpected replies and foresee unforeseen uses of our own words and ourselves by others. We would be more likely than others to recognize how even an admirer's repetition of our words may embarrass us and how another's reformulation of our meaning in the most alien terms may convert us. (791)

Ultimately, engaging consciously in the ongoing exchange of utterance and understanding would enable members of this community, like members of any community that recognizes and values dialogue, to understand themselves and what they know better as they learn from this process "not just what others may mean but what they themselves may mean among others" (792).

This is why Bakhtin argues throughout his work not only that communication is ontologically a dialogical process, but that it is only within this process that communication can function ethically by enabling us to decide what is true and what is not, what is good and what is not, and what we will, both individually and collectively, believe and do. Bakhtin's point throughout his work is that we must recognize this process as our reality and take responsibility for our actions within it as we construct together in the dialogue of our discourse the beliefs and values that determine our collective attitudes and cooperative actions. Only when we understand that using language is necessarily an act of collaboration through which we create the meaning we share, a socially constructed meaning that is inherently incomplete, only then can we speak and listen, write and read, responsibly. For Bakhtin, our greatest danger is that we might forget the essential answerability of the versions of the world that we or others have constructed, and in doing so stop the dialogue. Ultimately, his purpose is to remind us that:

> there is not first or last discourse, and dialogical context knows no limits (it disappears into an unlimited past and in our unlimited future). Even

past meanings . . . can never be stable (completed once and for all, finished), they will always change . . . in the course of the dialogue's subsequent development. . . . At every moment of the dialogue, there are immense and unlimited masses of forgotten meanings, but, in some subsequent moments, as the dialogue moves forward, they will return to memory and live in renewed form (in a new context). Nothing is absolutely dead: every meaning will celebrate its rebirth. The problem of the great temporality. (Todorov 110)

2

Rhetoric in Dialectic: The Functional Context of Writing

IN PRACTICE, OUR COMMUNICATION IS NECESSARILY SITUATED IN the social process of exchange that is described by dialogue. However, Chaim Perelman has reminded us that discourse can function in the context of dialogue for different purposes, including purposes that are not, as I have been using the term, dialogical ("The Dialectical Method" 164–65).[1] We can interact in dialogue for the purpose of discovering in our differing ideas points of agreement that will allow us to cooperate in the process of developing the shared knowledge that will support further cooperation. But we can also interact for the purpose of defeating ideas that differ from our own as we compete with others for power. In essence, the discourse we contribute to a dialogue can be propelled by purposes that are, in terms taken from Perelman, eristic or dialectical. When we assert as complete and absolute truth what is really but one interpretation, our discourse is eristic in its attempt to impose that interpretation upon others. But when we present an interpretation to others for them to judge, opening it to their modifying response, we contribute through our discourse to the kind of dialectical exchange that enables people to collaborate in discovering and validating what they can collectively consider true.

This distinction suggests that the term *dialogue* can be used to describe any exchange of assertions and responses, whereas the term *dialectic* is used to describe a particular kind of dialogue, one sustained exclusively for the purpose of constructing and revising knowledge that its participants can share.[2] Whether the discourse that contributes to dialogue is dialectical or eristic depends upon the purposes that propel it, purposes that are the concern of both Plato and Aristotle in their theoretical discussions of rhetoric that we continue to treat as fundamental. The conventional notion of rhetoric describes discourse that is eristic in its purpose, discourse that, as Plato described it in his *Gorgias*, would replace the collaborative dynamics of dialectic with a numbing manipulation. This notion places rhetoric and dialectic in the kind of direct opposition Stanley Fish once described: rhetoric "mirror[s] and present[s] for approval the opinions its readers already hold," whereas dialectic "requires of its readers a searching and rigorous scrutiny of everything they believe and live by" (*Self-Consuming Artifacts* 1). I read Plato's later *Phaedrus*, however, as less concerned with opposing rhetoric and dialectic than with distinguishing between two rhetorics of opposing purposes. Here Plato condemns discourse that is eristic in its purpose, that would undermine dialectic by stopping the process of exchange, in order to celebrate an alternative dialectical rhetoric describing discourse that contributes to the progress of an exchange that enables participants in a dialogue to collaborate in the process of constructing the shared interpretations that become their common knowledge.

I read the *Rhetoric* of Plato's student Aristotle as an attempt to formalize this notion of a dialectical rhetoric by analyzing rhetoric and dialectic as closely related applications of the dialectical reasoning people use when they attempt to decide together matters that cannot be demonstrated absolutely. For Aristotle, rhetoric and dialectic both describe processes of discursive exchange in which people cooperate in developing and validating shared knowledge. Whereas Aristotle's dialectic describes the disciplined and deliberate dialogue of specialists who use it to construct knowledge that is essentially theoretical, his rhetoric describes a more popular, pluralistic exchange, an essentially public dialogue that enables members of diverse communities to make the practical decisions that will support their collective action. But the differences between the two are less significant than the similarities. Indeed, in his modern revision of the *Rhetoric* Perelman preserves Aristotle's distinction between rhetoric and dialectic, yet renders it unimportant by describing dialectic as but a particular application of what he calls "a new rhetoric" that describes the dialectical function of "the whole range of discourse that aims at persuasion and conviction, whatever the audience addressed and whatever the subject matter" (*The Realm of Rhetoric* 5).

This dialectical notion of rhetoric is based upon assumptions about the nature of knowledge and language that are directly opposed to those that would support an eristic rhetoric.[3] Discourse that is eristic in its purpose treats knowledge as something we possess and language as the vehicle we use to transport what we know to others, assumptions demanding that content be separated from form and rhetoric be considered a matter of form and presentation alone. In contrast, discourse that is dialectical, as I will argue here that Plato and Aristotle both perceive it to be, treats knowledge as current consensual interpretations of common experience, and language as the activity of social interaction through which people develop those interpretations and share them. Further, whereas the assumptions that underlie an eristic rhetoric lend to the rhetor's voice the authority of one who has privileged access to truth, those underlying a dialectical rhetoric demand that any rhetor function as but one voice in a pluralistic process of collaborative exchange through which a community of equals discover and validate what they can collectively consider true.[4] An eristic rhetoric trains us in the art of authoritative statement; a dialectical rhetoric guides us in the process of coming to agreement. It continually reminds us that, in John Gage's terms, knowledge is an "activity" in which we participate with others through our discourse, and not a "commodity" that discourse carries from one person to another (156).

In the first chapter of this study I drew upon various disciplines, particularly literary theory, to describe the emerging recognition that writing functions as communication within the social context of a dialogical exchange. In this second chapter I am drawing upon classical rhetoric to describe that function as specifically dialectical. Taken together, Plato's discussion in the *Phaedrus* that describes the function of written discourse in the context of an ongoing dialectic and Aristotle's in the *Rhetoric* that describes the actual composition of writing within that context[5] provide us with a dialectical rhetoric that describes how written texts function constructively within our communities. Both emphasize that meaningful participation in written dialogues, whether as writers or readers of what someone else has written, requires of us a constant awareness and acknowledgment that writer and reader are equal partners in the process of making meaning; that it is always, in Gage's terms, "an active audience which motivates the composer's inquiry into possible knowledge, rather than a passive audience to which prior knowledge is meant to be passed on" (162).

Plato's Dialectical Rhetoric for Writing

Although Plato does not explain his notion of the dialectical function of writing until the end of the *Phaedrus,* all of what precedes that explanation prepares us for it. The dialogue begins with an exchange of speeches about love. The first is read to Socrates by Phaedrus from a text written by Lysias, and it is followed by two more that Socrates recites from what he describes as a textlike inspiration. As they discuss the issues raised by those speeches, Socrates and Phaedrus soon focus their attention on writing and, specifically, on the problem of distinguishing good writing from bad. It is in this discussion that Plato develops his description of a "true" dialectical rhetoric, a description he begins with an unconventional definition: "Rhetoric, taken as a whole," Socrates tells Phaedrus, "is an art of influencing the soul through words," one, he adds, that is used in private as well as in public to address matters that are "small" as well as those that are "great" (261). Phaedrus is surprised at this definition, because it expands rhetoric well beyond the techniques of public persuasion that he has so diligently studied until it seems to encompass all discourse, and because it asserts that rhetorical discourse is concerned with not just the practical and political, but also the matters of the soul, which are, as Plato uses the term *soul,* matters of truth. Throughout the rest of the dialogue Plato emphasizes that, above all, rhetoric in its "true nature" is concerned with moving people's constructions of their collective knowledge closer to the truth in which he persistently believes.

Despite the distance that separates Plato's conviction of a transcendent truth and the social constructionist commitment to a contingent reality, both rely on the same kind of dialectical exchange of discourse to provide people with the knowledge they need to live and act together. Plato's reliance on this collaborative function of rhetoric is embedded in his epistemology as it is summarized in

Socrates' second speech on love. Truth, he tells Phaedrus, is an entity our souls once witnessed but in their mortality have forgotten. All we retain are fragmentary memories accessible to us only through reasoning, which he defines as the process by which the soul remembers (249). Reasoning, however, is not something we can do alone. We are awakened to those memories only by the reasoned discourse of others that enables us to recognize there fragments of that truth. Only through this collaborative process of reasoned exchange can we begin to recover what we have forgotten and move closer to true knowledge. That is why Socrates prefers never to leave the city, why he tells Phaedrus, "Trees and countryside have no desire to teach me anything; it's only the men in the city that do" (230). Only when our memories are quickened by the discourse of others can we claim another fragment of what our souls remember, a fragment that, when extended by our own memories and presented in our discourse, can, in turn, quicken the memories of other souls. Because we come to know only through this dialectical exchange of discourse, and coming to know is, for Plato, the essential human act, the only rhetoric he can affirm is one in which we continually reconstruct our collective knowledge in a process that he believes moves it closer to the truth. That is why his Socrates proceeds to develop with Phaedrus a rhetoric that describes written discourse functioning within the context of an ongoing dialectic (269).[6]

Having posed the problem of distinguishing between good and bad writing, and having developed the outline of a dialectical rhetoric to provide the basis for that distinction, Plato begins the final section of the *Phaedrus* by Socrates' restating that problem for Phaedrus in explicitly Platonic terms: "Now do you know how to act or speak about words so that you may best please the gods?" (274), a question Socrates then answers in terms of writing alone. The *Phaedrus* is generally read as a critique of rhetoric and writing that affirms formal oral dialectic as the only true art of discourse. However, I read Plato as providing here a description of how written rhetorical discourse can and must function within the dynamic context of an ongoing and progressing dialogue.[7] This description condemns writing that is eristic in order to celebrate writing that is dialectical: writing that is thus made provisional, contingent, in Bakhtin's term, "answerable." As Jacques Derrida notes in his study of the *Phaedrus*, Plato provides here a description that "sav[es] writing" by "causing it to be lost" (67).

Socrates answers his own question about the kind of writing that would please the gods by creating a myth that describes its origin, a myth in which writing is condemned by a god. According to the myth, Theuth, the lesser god who invented writing, presented it to the greater god Thamus with the claim that it would make people wiser by improving their memories and thus is "a recipe for both memory and wisdom" (68). Derrida notes, however, that the word *recipe*, translated from the Greek *pharmakon*, can also mean "drug" in a sense that, to make Theuth's claim even more ambiguous, can mean either "remedy" or "poison." Indeed, when Thamus responds and refutes Theuth's claim, he does so by referring to writing as a drug that poisons:

> The fact is that this invention will produce forgetfulness in the souls of those who have learned it. They will not need to exercise their memories, being able to rely on what is written, calling things to mind no longer from within themselves by their own unaided powers, but under the stimulus of external marks that are alien to themselves. So it's not a recipe [drug] for memory, but for reminding, that you have discovered. And as for wisdom, you're equipping your pupils only with a semblance of it, not with truth. Thanks to you and your invention . . . they'll entertain the delusion that they have wide knowledge, while they are, in fact, for the most part incapable of real judgment. (275)

Writing does not please this god because he recognizes how readily a text can stop the process of dialectical exchange and, consequently, collective progress toward knowledge of the truth. A text presents what is an incomplete version of the truth but presents it as an entity that, because it is palpable and permanent, seems complete and thus authoritative. Consequently, a reader can allow the text she reads to supplant her need to continue the perpetual process of constructing the truth. That is a danger that Socrates and Phaedrus together acknowledged: "Is it not a fact," Socrates asked and Phaedrus agreed, that when a man writes with sufficient force to become "an immortal author in his own country," he then "regards himself as an equal of the gods and that posterity cherishes this same opinion about him when it inspects his writings?" (258).

But because no mortal can, like the gods, see and know the truth, any mortal representation of truth must be inherently incomplete. Yet, writing presents to its readers a text that not only affirms its own completeness but, because a text fixes its statement outside the social context in which it was generated, seemingly declares itself as autonomous, as removed from the modifying process of dialectical exchange. When a writer claims truth or when truth is attributed to a writer's text by a reader, a text becomes a kind of poison that replaces the dynamic process of collaborative reasoning with a counterfeit truth, one that then supplants for us the essential acts of questioning and remembering. As Derrida describes it, writing substitutes what is "passive" and "mechanical" for "the active reanimation of knowledge" so that "instead of quickening life in the original" it "can at best restore only its monuments" (108–9).

This poison has, in Derrida's word, its "antidote" in the dialectical process that keeps all discourse, including written texts, suspended in a critical, collaborative exchange where it is subjected to the process of "mutual questioning and self-examination" that continually reminds its participants of the incomplete and provisional nature of any assertion. Going through this process, Plato believed, would propel its participants' progress toward knowledge of truth (121). Consequently, when a text is suspended in an ongoing dialectic we recognize what the text itself would allow us to forget, that, as Socrates tells Phaedrus, "the written word on any subject necessarily contains much that is playful, and . . . no word, whether in verse or prose, has ever been written or recited that is worthy of serious attention" (277). This is important because every text is necessarily temporary, necessarily engaged in the process of, in Derrida's words, "sustaining itself in living dialogue" (154). And it is only within this "living dialogue" that writing can function not as a poison but, consistent with Theuth's claim, as a remedy for our faulty memories that contributes to our wisdom by freeing us from the constant necessity to remember all that we have already learned. We can then engage our minds more vigorously in the dialectical process of constructing what is new and, as we do so, return continually to the textual record of what we have learned to reassess and modify what we know (Burger 1–2). Most importantly, however, writing remedies the restrictions that limit participation in the dialectical process by recording versions of truth in texts that open that process of exchange to participants who are removed from us in space and time, broadening the base of our collaboration and making the whole process more fruitful.

Consequently, knowledge that emerges from the epistemic interaction of a written dialectic can, in Plato's terms, present current and validated "lessons in justice and beauty and goodness which are delivered for the sake of true instruction, which are, in fact, inscribed in the soul," and only such lessons as these are "worthy to be implanted in the souls of others" (278). Sharing such knowledge is, for Plato, "the serious pursuit of the dialectician: to find "a congenial soul" and then "with true knowledge" born of memory and reason "plant and sow" there words "which can transmit their seed to other natures and cause the growth of fresh words in them . . . ," collaboratively constructed words that propel the progress of a community's shared knowledge (276–77). This is the revisionist notion of writing that Plato's Socrates asks Phaedrus to carry back to the school of Lysias, a notion in which both writers and readers would treat every text as necessarily partial and provisional. Socrates' message is this: "If a man composes his work with the full knowledge of the truth and can come to the aid of what he has written when he is challenged and has the power to demonstrate from his own mouth the poverty of his writings, he ought not to be designated by a name drawn from them, but by one that indicates his serious pursuits . . . a lover of wisdom" (73–74).

Indeed, writers and readers who love wisdom know only one truth: that every text is incomplete. Only when a text is suspended in the process of the constant, collaborative exchange that is dialectic can writing, a drug that can poison the knowledge of those who misuse it, provide a remedy for the limits that time, space, and memory put upon our ability to revise and refine what we know. When writing is situated within the process of dialectic, texts are made temporary despite their authoritative appearance. The permanence that poisons them is lost when texts are treated as nothing more than transcriptions of statements made in response to other statements, as temporary and provisional interpretations that are submitted to the modifying judgment of others. It is the power of texts to preserve a record of that process that makes writing a gift from the gods, a gift that allows us to extend the process of dialectical interaction beyond the immediate boundaries of time and place and to trace the history of our judgments and judge them again in the continual process of constructing and reconstructing the knowledge that supports our collective life.

Aristotle's Process of Dialectical Writing

Whereas Plato describes why writing must function within the context of an ongoing process of dialectical exchange, Aristotle describes how it does so. In the first line of his *Rhetoric,* Aristotle defines his term by stating that "rhetoric is the counterpart of dialectic" (1354a), a statement William M. A. Grimaldi suggests would be better translated by replacing the term *counterpart* with *analogue* (56). What this statement suggests is that, for Aristotle, dialectic and rhetoric are different applications of what is essentially the same process of exchange that people use to establish agreements they can treat as knowledge. For Aristotle, then, the purpose of discourse that is rhetorical is identical to the purpose of discourse in dialectic: to engage people in a process of collaborative exchange through which they can judge together what they will collectively consider good or true.[8] Rhetoric, in his description, differs from dialectic not in purpose or function but in materials and participants: dialectic is an exchange sustained by a few specialists for the purpose of establishing specialized knowledge or general theoretical principles in contingent matters, whereas rhetoric is a similar exchange sustained publicly within larger and more complex communities for the purpose of establishing collective values and assumptions and deciding upon collective actions.[9]

When Aristotle defines rhetoric as "the faculty of observing in any given case the available means of persuasion" and identifies its function as "discern[ing] the real and the apparent means of persuasion just as it is the function of dialectic to discern the real and apparent syllogism" (1355b), he is saying that rhetoric is the public and popular analogue of the dialectic that smaller communities of people use to establish and extend the shared knowledge upon which they base their more immediate cooperation. Consequently, Aristotle's rhetoric differs from his dialectic primarily in the directness and immediacy of the interaction allowed its participants. Because participants in rhetorical interactions are separated from each other by circumstances, space, and time—as in public gatherings where speaker and listeners are separated by both distance and the number of people who are audience, or in the writing and reading of a text, in which writer and reader are separated by time and space— the actual interactional process of establishing and extending shared knowledge cannot be situated in the kind of intimate, step-by-step negotiation that characterizes dialectic. Instead, the rhetor must simulate that negotiative exchange in the process of composition itself and propose its outcome in speech or text to the audience for their assent.

Such a proposal is what Aristotle calls an *enthymeme*, which he describes as "the substance" (1354a) and "means" (1355b) of persuasion. An enthymeme functions in a rhetorical exchange as a syllogism functions in dialectic: as a proposition to be collaboratively tested. It does so by affirming the knowledge that rhetor and audience currently share and by asserting on that basis a potential extension or application of that knowledge. If the audience accepts that assertion, they are persuaded; if they do not, the rhetor must modify the proposition in terms of their response. That is how rhetoric is, for Aristotle, the process of "observing" or "discerning" ideas or concepts that have the potential to become shared knowledge through the interaction of discourse. Rhetoric describes the process of testing various possibilities in a dialectical process of exchange until a rhetor can articulate a possibility that an audience can accept.

As such, the enthymeme is more than an incomplete syllogism for which the audience must supply the missing term because the audience retains the power to accept or reject its assertion. And it is more than a simple statement of assumptions that rhetor and audience share, because its composition embodies the moment in which new knowledge is first constructed. Enthymemes embody the collaborative interaction of rhetor and audience itself, an interaction that is provisionally simulated when the enthymeme is initially composed but is then made actual when that enthymeme is presented to the audience for their judgment. Because it must emerge in what Grimaldi terms "the confrontation of speaker and audience" as a proposition of potential shared knowledge, the enthymeme cannot be purely the invention of the rhetor (58). As Gage puts it, an enthymeme is essentially a compromise between what one person wants to assert and what others are willing to accept (157–58).

Aristotle's emphasis on the enthymeme supports Plato's claim that rhetorical discourse, whether spoken or written, should function within the context of a dialectical exchange where it is subjected to the judgment and modification of others. But it also makes explicit what Plato only implied, that rhetorical discourse is actually composed *within* that process of exchange. We construct the enthymemes we will propose in full consciousness of those we will use them to address, doing so in a simulated dialectic that allows us to anticipate what versions of reality our audience might accept. In Kenneth Burke's terms, constructing an enthymeme requires us to identify ourselves with others by coming to share with them an apprehension of reality, and that identification is an act he places at the center of all our discourse (*Attitudes Toward History* 267). Dialectic, as Burke describes it, involves responding to "division" with a "retreat to a level of terms that allow some kind of merger (as 'near' and 'far' are merged into the concept of distance)" in order to "'return' to the division, now seeing it as pervaded by the spirit of the 'One' we had found in our retreat" (*A Grammar of Motives* 440). It is in this process of identifying ourselves with others that we find the enthymemes that define our common ground and articulate the way it might be extended.

This act of identification is at the center of rhetoric as Burke defines it—"the use of language as a symbolic means of inducing cooperation"—because what every rhetorical exchange articulates is the shared knowledge that provides the basis for cooperation (*A Rhetoric of Motives* 43). For Burke the process of communication cannot begin until we identify ourselves with others—in some way identifying our ways with theirs (55)—in order to find a point of anticipated agreement that we express in the enthymeme that functions as a proposal for compromise: "the rhetorician may have to change an audience's opinion in one respect," notes Burke, "but he can succeed only insofar as he yields to that audience's opinions in other respects" (56). Consequently, the dialectical interaction of rhetor and audience is first enacted by the rhetor alone in the process of composing an enthymeme. That makes composition itself a dialectical process through which we change our own perceptions of shared knowledge as we adapt them to the language and attitudes of those we will address. The enthymemes that our rhetoric expresses must emerge from the private process of reconstructing our own knowledge in reference to others, the first step in the public process of coming to agreement. When we compose rhetorical discourse we attempt, in Burkean terms, to identify ourselves with our perception of what those we will address believe and might believe, and in doing so we necessarily change what we believe in the process.

Whereas Plato's dialectical rhetoric describes the functions of written discourse within the dialectical exchange of assertions and responses where knowledge is collaboratively constructed, Aristotle's rhetoric describes the composition of those assertions within the preliminary dialectical interaction that is sustained within the mind of the rhetor. And that is why Aristotle's *Rhetoric*, focusing as it does on the enthymeme, is a treatise on invention, on the process of finding and asserting for the judgment of others some extension or application of knowledge already shared. Because the act of writing itself is generally performed in isolation, where a writer works alone in the process of creating a text, we assume that writing is a solitary act. But the insights that Aristotle provides on the social context in which the process of constructing an enthymeme is situated emphasize that even the act of composition itself is inherently dialectical—the point Bakhtin made, as well—and that writing is inherently a collaborative act in which writer and reader construct together a version of knowledge that is in some way new to them both.

Dialectical Writing and Dialectical Reading

A text, removing both writer and reader as it does from any immediate interaction, is necessarily enthymemic: it must attribute to its readers their acceptance of the assumptions and agreements it presents even though those assumptions and agreements are provisional and subject to their judgment. Recognizing that our texts inhabit this uncertain ground between assertion and acceptance requires us both to write them and to read them in ways that will keep them suspended in the ongoing process of collaborative judgment that is described by dialectic. In other words, the notion that written texts function in the context of a dialectical exchange requires us to write and to read in full recognition that our partners in the process, the writers we are reading or the readers to whom we write, are our necessary collaborators in the making of meaning.

Aristotle's discussion of the enthymeme describes how we enact this suspension in the process of composing, how the writer must judge and modify her ideas in ways she anticipates her readers might accept. Rhetoric, to Aristotle, is this art of composing and presenting potential shared knowledge. Because his rhetoric is essentially "preparatory for judgment and action," in Grimaldi's words, it should be understood as "the ability to perceive and to present evidence which makes decision, and a definite decision, possible; but to stop with presentation" (27). Plato's discussion in the *Phaedrus* of the dialectical function of written texts explains why writers must place what they write in such suspension. Knowledge is a process, a matter of motion, but texts, he has Socrates tell Phaedrus, are static and thus inherently unresponsive to the dynamic reconstructive process of dialectic. "Once a thing is put in writing," Socrates continues, "it rolls about all over the place, falling into the hands of those who have no concern with it just as easily as under the notice of those who comprehend" (275). A text that is written with the assumption that it describes things as they actually are, that it tells the truth, is, then, necessarily a disgrace to its writer (277). Instead, every text must be written in full recognition of its "poverty," of the inherent incompleteness and error that are born of the temporality of its writer (278).

Further, Socrates contends, readers must confront texts with that same recognition, for even if its writer recognizes its limitations, a text can remain part of the dialectical process only as long as its readers keep it suspended there. We are "utterly simple-minded" if we believe that "any subject will be clear or certain because it is couched in writing," if we believe that "words put in writing are something more than what they are in fact: a reminder to [those] already conversant with the subject, of the material with which the writing is concerned" (275). On the other hand, we are wise if we remember that "the written word on any subject necessarily contains much that is playful," that no text has ever been written "that is worthy of serious attention" (277). Readers who remember that will read every text, including Plato's *Phaedrus*, dialectically, treating each as nothing more than a provisional representation of truth and submitting each, whether or not the text invites it, to the process of judgment that results in its refutation, modification, or revision. Reading such as this is essential to the process of collaboration through an exchange of texts that is the textual counterpart of Plato's oral dialectic. Rhetoric, in Aristotle's description, has two functions: first, "to discover the means of coming as near [success in persuading] as the circumstances of each particular case allow," and second, "to discern the real and the apparent means of persuasion, just as it is the function of dialectic to discern the real and apparent syllogism" (1355b). These two parallel functions, the first concerned more with the process of composing and the second suggesting the process of critical reading, demonstrate that in written rhetoric, as in oral dialectic, both classes of participants in the exchange, writers and readers, contribute to the process of constructing shared knowledge.

When we suspend the texts we write and read in the collaborative context described by a dialectical rhetoric, we eliminate at once the two fictions that pervade the way we think about and use writing: the fiction of the autonomous writer and the fiction of the passive reader. Guided by a dialectical rhetoric we both write and read as a part of a process in which we must, as Gadamer puts it in *Truth and Method*, "accept the priority of the question over the answer" (328), thereby exercising "the art of asking questions" and preserving an "orientation towards openness" that he describes as "the art of conducting a real conversation" (330). No one tries to control the process or direct the progress of conversations that persist. Instead, participants allow themselves "to be conducted by the object to which the partners in the conversation are directed," and that object is what Plato called the "voyage of discourse" they have embarked upon together (Gadamer 330). When that is the way we read and write, we bring every text "back out of the alienation in which it finds itself and into the living presence of conversation, whose fundamental procedure is always question and answer" (331).

3

Writing in Conversation: The Conversation Model

PEOPLE WORKING IN COMPOSITION STUDIES HAVE, OVER THE LAST decade, been exploring the function of the activities of writing and reading as parts of the dialogical, dialectical process through which the shared knowledge that supports cooperation is collaboratively constructed. In doing so, we follow theorists from a variety of disciplinary perspectives who have described this meaning-making process as a kind of conversation. Martin Heidegger, for example, wrote, "our being . . . is founded in language" and language "only becomes actual in conversation," an activity he defined as "speaking with others about something" for the purpose of bringing about "the process of coming together." From this definition, Heidegger could argue, "conversation and its unity support our existence" and, indeed, "we . . . are a conversation" (301). And although this is the process Martin Buber described as dialogue, he used the term *conversation* to suggest his notion of the ideal dialogue. For Buber, "genuine conversation" is a dialogue in which each participant "has in mind the other or others in their present and particular being and turns to them with the intention of establishing a living mutual relationship between himself and them" (Friedman 87). Such a conversation requires participation without "abbreviation and distortion" and "without appearance," participation characterized by the willingness of participants to submit themselves fully to this collaborative process of meaning making without knowing where it will lead.

Michael Oakeshott, brought to the attention of many of us by Kenneth Bruffee's essay "Collaborative Learning and the 'Conversation of Mankind,'" also presented conversation as "the appropriate image" to describe the social context in which our discourse functions. Like Heidegger, Oakeshott argued that we can make meaning only in terms of our social experience, only in the context of the unity and the continuity that we cooperatively define through shared discourse. In his essay "The Voice of Poetry in the Conversation of Mankind," Oakeshott observed that although formal argument might be a part of that process—although it might characterize particular "passages" of a conversation—most participation is more spontaneous, more informal than argument, carried on as it is almost continuously among equals and progressing as it does almost always without any authoritative agenda. This free conversation provides the context that enables us to attach both meaning to "human activity and utterance" and value to "practical enterprise and intellectual achievement" (198–99).

Perhaps the most familiar use of the term *conversation* to describe the meaning-making exchange in which human discourse functions is Kenneth Burke's. Burke argued in *The Philosophy of Literary Form* that we must learn to treat any discourse and, particularly, any written discourse as an action someone takes in response to a particular set of circumstances. In his words, we must read every text "as a strategy for encompassing a situation" and, consequently, as an "answer or rejoinder" to texts that have preceded it (109). To help us understand what he means, Burke described the social context within which the texts we read and write have their function with a memorable portrait of what he called "an unending conversation":

> Imagine that you enter a parlor. You come late. When you arrive, others have long preceded you, and they are engaged in a heated discussion, a discussion too heated for them to pause and tell you exactly what it is about. In fact, the discussion had already begun long before any of them got there, so that no one present is qualified to retrace for you all the steps that had gone before. You listen for a while until you decide that you have caught the tenor of the argument; then you put in your oar. Someone answers; you answer him; another comes to your defense; another aligns himself against you. . . . However, the discussion is interminable. The hour grows late, you must depart. And you do depart, with the discussion still in progress. (110–11)

For Burke, what is essential about the functional context of writing is that it is such a conversation that is continuous in time. It is a process that people may join and people may leave, but one that requires each person's contribution to respond to what others have contributed before. Through this process individual interpretations of meaning are continuously exchanged and revised as people construct together interpretations they can share.

Based upon the terminology provided by statements like these, theoretical discussions in composition have begun to use the concept of conversation metaphorically to describe the social circumstances in which writing makes meaning. The purpose of this chapter is to synthesize and build upon that work by describing what has come to be called the conversation model for the social context in which writing functions. In doing so, I must first summarize recent research in communication studies that describes the social function of oral conversation, as well as review the notion of discourse communities developed by people in composition studies to describe the social structures within which written conversations are sustained, work that demonstrates that any conversation—whether carried on in speech or in writing—must be situated within a community. On that basis I will then discuss how the notion of conversation can describe the social context in which written discourse has both meaning and purpose, doing so in terms of the description of the social function of discourse provided by Lloyd Bitzer in his theory of rhetorical situation.

Conversation Theory, Rhetoric, and Writing

During the last decade, work in composition studies has frequently described the social function of writing in terms of the most common social context in which speech functions, conversation.[1] Elaine Maimon used that term in 1979 when she suggested that students might write more successfully in school if they understood that when they produce academic discourse they are, in effect, entering a conversation in progress where their discourse must conform to assumptions about knowledge and form that are already established among its participants. Charles Bazerman used the term again in 1980 when he proposed "the conversational model" as a way to describe how what we write is situated within the context of what we have read, and how our writing, like our speech in a conversation, builds upon the form and content we have encountered in the discourse of others in a way that "advances the total sum of discourse" (658). More recently, Kenneth Bruffee has drawn upon Oakeshott as well as Clifford Geertz and Stanley Fish in using the term to connect written and oral discourse and to argue, "if thought is internalized public and social talk, then writing of all kinds is internalized social talk made public and social again," and that makes writing "a technologically displaced form of conversation" (641).

What this use of the term *conversation* suggests is that any text must function within the larger context of a succession of texts that respond to each other in the process of defining knowledge that the community of people who read and write them can share. Although this notion seems intuitively valid and generally consistent with theoretical assumptions drawn from the various disciplines upon which current work in composition is based, it has been only informally described. My initial purpose here is to describe it more formally by using terms derived from conversation theory as it is being assembled by researchers in interpersonal communication and from the notion of rhetorical conversation as it is being described by theorists in rhetoric.

Current theory in oral conversation is founded upon the fundamental recognition, stated by Berger and Luckman in *The Social Construction of Reality*, that people engage in conversation for the purpose of coordinating their separate interpretations of experience to establish shared meanings:

> The most important vehicle of reality-maintenance is conversation. . . . At the same time that the conversational apparatus ongoingly maintains reality, it ongoingly *modifies* it. . . . Thus the fundamental reality-maintaining fact is the continuing use of the same language to objectify unfolding biographical experience. In the widest sense, all who employ this same language are reality-maintaining others. (172–73)

This statement describes the fundamental nature of conversation: not only does it function socially to create the common conception of reality upon which cooperation can be based, but the very process of sustaining it requires members of a community to participate in an exchange in which those conceptions are continuously revised and extended. In its essence, conversation is a cooperative endeavor sustained upon a foundation of shared meanings for the purpose of establishing further shared meanings that will support further co-operation and, thus, further conversation.[2]

In *Communicative Acts and Shared Knowledge in Natural Discourse*, Marga Kreckel describes conversation as a kind of negotiative process in which people successively submit their interpretations of meaning to the modifying judgment of others for the sake of constructing an interpretation they can share. Through this exchange of assertion and response a group of individuals is able to collaborate in constructing what she calls "shared knowledge," the term I have used throughout this study.[3] According to Kreckel, we are motivated to join a conversation when we find we have particular needs and purposes in common with others and recognize that these needs can be met and these purposes fulfilled only through cooperation. Because cooperation can be maintained only on the basis of shared knowledge, we must each subject our private "concept" of meaning to the mediation of the conversational process in order to assemble the collectively held meanings that will support collective action (27). This shared knowledge not only provides the materials that enable people to sustain this process; it also constitutes the product of the exchange, making it both the means and the end of the conversation.

An essential characteristic of this process is that it is situated in time. Once begun, conversations are structured in a sequence of turn-taking whose participants present individual interpretations of knowledge already shared to the process of revision and reconstruction that is sustained in the current exchange.[4] The goal of each participant at any point in this process is to bring her individual interpretation into correspondence with the interpretations of the others. Through conversational exchange the diverse interpretations of participants come into closer correspondence, and the shared knowledge that sustains further conversation is changed.

Can this description of conversation as the social context in which speech transforms both individual meanings and shared knowledge provide a model for the social context in which writing functions? Thomas B. Farrell has examined the relationship of conversation and rhetoric—of, essentially, speech and writing—in terms that suggest that it can. For him, conversation is an "informal exchange of utterances" ("Aspects of Coherence in Conversation and Rhetoric" 262) that has two characteristics: what he calls "reciprocity," an interactive pattern of assertion and response, and "continual movement," a progressing "sense of passage" (264–65). On the other hand, rhetoric is more deliberate discourse in which "agreements" that will support cooperation are "formed or anticipated." "Rhetoric," Farrell emphasizes, "emerges in discourse as a reflective and anticipatory choice among options that are imposed upon us in a moment of uncertain contingency" (262). But although these definitions contrast, they do not necessarily contradict. Indeed, conversation as Farrell describes it—a reciprocal exchange of discourse that results in a progressing sense of shared meaning—has the dialogical and dialectical characteristics of conversation as described by Kreckel and other theorists, and of rhetoric as described by Plato and Aristotle.

As the terms of his definition of rhetoric suggest, Farrell distinguishes conversation and rhetoric primarily on the basis of what conversation lacks and rhetoric has: a "still moment of contingent choice" in which "we abandon our equation of spontaneous thought with expression in favor of a more deliberate interpretive horizon— of proposal and attendance, of advocacy and audience" (272). In developing this distinction, Farrell distinguishes between conversation and rhetoric in terms of time. In conversation, utterance is generally spontaneous and rhetorical discourse tends to be premeditated (262). Consequently, conversation develops according to the "spontaneous reciprocation and synthesis of participants," whereas rhetoric develops more deliberately in order to address "some zone of uncertain difference upon which discussion comes to rest." Because conversation is guided by an intention that is "emergent," whereas rhetoric is guided by an intention that is "proposed" (269), the influence of the discourse of conversation upon the knowledge of a community is often "perishable"; that of rhetorical discourse can be more "lasting" (267–69).

But the similarity Farrell finds in the tendency of both conversation and rhetoric to invite the responses and restatements of others, to invite critical dialogue, is more significant than these differences (267). What he describes as rhetoric seems to emerge within the context of a conversation when the interaction is deliberately directed at developing some sort of agreement about meanings, when people who converse consciously collaborate in the process of constructing shared knowledge.[5] For Farrell, conversation becomes rhetorical when participants begin to judge each other's messages in terms of knowledge they can share and upon which they can continue to converse and, thus, cooperate (275). Consequently, ordinary conversation is transformed into rhetorical conversation when participants become a cooperating community comprising individuals, who must each, in Farrell's words, "suspend (for the time being) his or her individual biases and alignments in favor of a more critical attitude toward potentially generalizable interests" (277).

What rhetorical theorists are calling rhetorical conversation is ordinary conversation transformed as people begin to present and to judge individual interpretations of shared knowledge for the express purpose of revising, extending, and improving a common interpretation.[6] In other words, conversation that has become rhetorical requires that its participants exercise active critical judgment in exchanging discourse that would contribute to the formation of some consensus. When such deliberation becomes a part of the conversational process, that process itself becomes more deliberate, taking more time as people consider critically what has been said and prepare a constructive response. Although the direction in which such conversations lead still emerges in the process rather than being proposed at the beginning, these acts of deliberation invoke intention. And because, according to general conversation theory, people use the exchange that term describes to define the common meanings, the shared knowledge, upon which they can build their future cooperation, it seems that most conversations, at some level of their social function, are, as Farrell uses the term, rhetorical.

In an important sense, time is what distinguishes speech and writing as they function in conversation: because expression and reception in writing are separated in time there is more time for each, more time to prepare the expression of an intention and more time to judge the message received. Relying as it does on these terms of time, Farrell's description of rhetoric seems to describe writing. Because conversation can become rhetorical when engaged in the construction of shared knowledge, writing might be considered conversational when it contributes to that process. That is, just as conversation describes the social process in which speech is made meaningful and functions within a community to create further meaning, the process of conversation also describes the social context in which writing is made meaningful and functions constructively within a collaborative process of meaning making.

Discourse Communities in Composition Studies

In composition studies, the social structure in which writing functions is described as a discourse community: as a group of people who use discourse according to agreed-upon rules to maintain a body of knowledge that will support their common efforts. This notion of the discourse community is based upon an understanding of knowledge and society that is shared by most significant contemporary observers of our communication, one described succinctly by Perelman and Olbrechts-Tyteca in *The New Rhetoric:*

> All language is language of a community, be this a community bound by biological ties, or by the practice of a common discipline or technique. The terms used, their definition, can only be understood in the context of the habits, ways of thought, methods, external circumstances, and traditions known to the users of those terms. . . . An agreement on the use of terms, no less than an agreement about the conception of reality and the vision of the world . . . is not indisputable; it is linked to a social and historical situation which fundamentally conditions any distinction that one might wish to discuss between judgments of reality and value judgments. (513)

Within this context of community, as they describe it, language is used to negotiate agreements that will support cooperation. Such negotiation necessitates choices that are posed and made through a rhetorical exchange.

The notion of discourse communities has become central to the work of people in composition as we have tried to determine what it is we need to teach our students when we teach them to write and, more fundamentally, why we are teaching them to write at all. It is not, however, a notion that is new. In fact, the concept that rhetoric functions within a community of people who collaborate in meeting collective needs and fulfilling collective purposes is implicit throughout the rhetorical tradition and its emphasis upon discourse that addresses others for the purpose of proposing choices concerning beliefs that the community comprising rhetor and audience might together adopt and actions they might collectively take. This is public discourse, discourse that addresses the beliefs and actions of a community—essentially, its public issues—and that makes its social function primarily political.[7]

This is the function of rhetoric Lloyd Bitzer describes in his essay "Rhetoric and Public Knowledge." Here Bitzer defines a community of people who use rhetoric to address such issues as "a public," a term taken from John Dewey, one of the philosophers of American pragmatism who, with Charles Sanders Pierce and Josiah Royce, understood knowledge and values to exist primarily among people who share common interpretations of experience.[8] Bitzer uses this notion to describe a community in which rhetoric functions to construct "public knowledge," which he defines as "that set of truths and values which would characterize a competent public" (83). His argument in this essay is that a group "of persons united in interests, aspirations, tradition, and experience" (74) that "alter in composition and nature according to the circumstances of their historic contexts" (79) must sustain a process of rhetorical exchange in order to maintain the knowledge that enables its members to agree and collaborate in response to change, a process constituted of discourse that "will enrich the public's information, sustain its experiential knowledge, and provide modes of debate and discussion needed for intelligent decision and action" (80). This is *public discourse* as I am using the term, and this process, ongoing within a community in which that discourse has its public function, is essentially the process I am calling *conversation.*

For people working in composition studies, Patricia Bizzell has provided perhaps the most useful examination of how writing functions within a discourse community. Specifically, her work addresses how we might better introduce our students into the academic discourse community—the immediate one in which their writing must function—but what she emphasizes is how people use writing to define and extend the shared knowledge that supports any community.[9] In her 1982 article, "Cognition, Convention, and Certainty: What We Need to Know about Writing," Bizzell described the constant exchange of discourse through which people organize and interpret their experience as a process that resembles conversation as I have been describing it: "This interaction modifies reasoning, speaking, and writing within society. Groups of society members can become accustomed to modifying each other's reasoning and language use in certain ways. Eventually these familiar ways achieve the status of conventions that bind the group in a discourse community, at work together on some project of interaction with the material world" (214). Bizzell also emphasized that because this interaction is situated in time, the knowledge that defines a discourse community is continually revised in the process of conversation, revalidated by a kind of progressing acceptance, or "rhetorical closure," that she calls consensus (226).

More recently, Bizzell has argued that the kind of written conversation that sustains this process is directed at mediating the conflict between a state of consensus and a statement that proposes how that consensus might be revised.[10] Such conversation comprises individual texts that each create for its participants a moment of choice—the primary characteristic of what Farrell calls rhetorical conversation. Writing that contributes to rhetorical conversation contributes to a process sustained within a community to resolve the conflicts inherent in the distance that separates any state of knowledge and the constantly changing circumstances of those who share it, each text presenting for judgment a revised version of shared knowledge that might mediate that conflict. Such discourse is clearly rhetorical in the Aristotelian sense, in which, in Grimaldi's words, rhetoric "is the ability to perceive and present evidence which makes decision, and a definite decision, possible" (27). When the function of a text is public because it enables deliberate choice among members of a community in matters that address shared knowledge and collective purpose, that text is rhetorical. When it is situated within the historical context of an exchange that is sustained within a community for the purpose of revising that knowledge in order to fulfill those purposes, that rhetoric is conversational.

Conversation as Context for the Rhetorical Situation

In his essay "The Will to Interpret," Josiah Royce described the function of discourse within communities in maintaining the changing body of shared knowledge that sustains the coherence of community life. For Royce, a community that attempts to achieve agreement in knowledge or action is necessarily a "community of interpretation" consisting of at least three persons: an interpreter, a person whose "mind" is to be interpreted, and a listener to whom the interpretation is to be addressed (315). The "office" of the first of these, the interpreter, is always "to conform to the mind which he interprets, and to the comprehension of the mind to which he addresses his interpretation" (317).

Royce's description of this social configuration in which an interpretation contributes to the development of shared knowledge seems to anticipate Lloyd Bitzer's description of the rhetorical situation. In two influential essays, the first published in 1968 and the second in 1980, Bitzer described rhetoric as discourse that is generated within the set of social circumstances he called a rhetorical situation and that functions there to change them.[11] The rhetorical situation, as Bitzer first described it, is "a natural context of persons, events, objects, relations, and an exigence which strongly invites utterance" (1968, 5); described more completely in 1980, it is a "complex of persons, events, objects, and relations which presents an exigence that can be completely or partially removed if discourse—introduced into the situation—can influence audience thought or action so as to bring about positive modification of the exigence" (24). Rhetorical discourse functions pragmatically within that situational context when the "rhetor alters reality by bringing into existence a discourse of such a character that the audience, in thought and action, is so engaged that it becomes a mediator of change" (1968, 4). In this way rhetoric brings people together in the shared knowledge that will support cooperation.

The particular constituents of the rhetorical situation as Bitzer defines it are three: exigence, audience, and constraints. A rhetorical exigence is a shared need, "an imperfection marked by urgency" (1968, 6), a "problem or defect, something other than it should be" (1980, 23) that can be modified through the discourse one individual addresses to others: "an audience capable of being constrained in thought or actions in order to effect positive modification of the exigence" (1980, 23), of cooperating as "mediators of change" (1968, 7). Bitzer describes the third constituent, constraints, as "persons, events, objects, and relations which are parts of the situation because they have the power to constrain decision and action needed to modify the exigence" (1968, 8); as "rules, principles, facts, laws, images, interests, emotions, arguments, and conventions" that, "having the power to influence decision and action needed to modify the exigence, . . . are parts of the situation and influence both the rhetor and audience" (1980, 23). In other words, constraints are those elements present in a rhetorical situation that are "capable of influencing the rhetor and an audience." They are, in essence, the "opportunities and limitations" that constitute the social context within which that situation is defined and the discourse generated there must function (1980, 23).

Royce's notion of communities of interpretation provides us with a description of the larger context in which a particular rhetorical situation, as Bitzer characterizes it, is itself situated. Specifically, Royce's notion places the individual moments of interpretation that sustain a community—the particular circumstances in which discourse emerges to draw people together in shared meanings— within that community's history of interpretation: "for at any moment, in my life as interpreter, I am dependent on the results of countless previous efforts to interpret. The whole past history of civilization has resulted in that form and degree of interpretation of you and of my other fellow-men which I already possess, at any instant when I begin afresh the task of interpreting your life and ideas" (314). Each of these moments of interpretation is a rhetorical situation, one that is connected not only to those that preceded it but to those that will follow. This continuity makes any act of interpretation part of a larger interpretive process, an ongoing exchange of interpretations that enables people to collaborate in developing one they can share. In Royce's description, each act of interpretation takes place within the context of an exchange that has the characteristics of conversation:

> We shall be many selves with a common ideal future event at which we aim. Without essentially altering the nature of our community, our respective offices can be, at our pleasure, interchanged. You, or my other neighbor, can at any moment assume the function of interpreter; while I pass to a new position in the new community. And yet, we three shall constitute as clearly as before a Community of Interpretation. The new community will be in a perfectly definite relation to the former one; and may grow out of it by a process as definite as is every form of conscious interpretation. (316)

Bitzer's analysis of rhetorical situation does not directly address this larger social context in which rhetorical situations exist.[12] Indeed, because his model describes the particular circumstances in which rhetorical discourse is *generated*, it offers only "part of a theory of situation" (1968, 3). His rhetorical situation describes the immediate components of the particular social circumstances within which rhetorical invention occurs, without describing the larger process of exchange that constrains invention and within which the discourse that is invented must function. Rhetorical situation as Bitzer describes it is isolated from its larger social context for the purpose of description. The description of the conversation model I am developing here describes the larger context of rhetorical interaction in which rhetorical situations are located, and within which rhetorical discourse finds its social function.

This larger context can be described as a conversation in which the discourses that address a succession of related rhetorical situations are embedded.[13] In Bitzer's terms, any exigence that can be defined within a community has a history, and members of that community who qualify as an audience to be addressed have some notion of that history. Consequently, the function of any rhetorical discourse within a community is necessarily constrained by the related discourses that have preceded it, that have, in a sequence of assertions and responses, contributed to the present state of shared knowledge that discourse would address. This constraining chain of past discourse—this historical conversation—is the larger context within which a rhetorical situation is itself situated and within which the discourse that addresses that situation must function constructively.[14]

Whereas the model of a rhetorical situation describes the immediate social context in which an individual rhetorical statement is generated, the model of a historical conversation describes the social context in which that statement has its public function. In terms of writing, the constituents of a historical conversation are the individual texts that, over time, address the particular needs and knowledge shared by a community of writers and readers. Neither written nor read in isolation, each is a response to others that preceded it, a product of a continuing collaborative effort. Each presents one writer's notion of how shared knowledge might be extended to readers for their judgment and response, responding to prior writing by presenting an assertion to which subsequent writing must respond. In this way, the texts we write and read redefine over time the very "persons, events, objects, relations, rules, principles, facts, laws, images, interests, emotions, arguments, and conventions" that, according to Bitzer, constrain what we can write and think. These constraining "opportunities and limitations" that reflect the current state of shared knowledge within a community are continuously revised in the conversations we sustain to resolve our conflicts and expand our cooperation. As we participate in these conversations, we make the texts we write and read function within our communities as public discourse.

Writing as Conversation

In *Philosophy and the Mirror of Nature* (1979), Richard Rorty synthesizes the views of contemporary philosophers who argue that we use language not so much to discover truth as to construct, situated as we are, what we call knowledge. Rorty's thesis is based on the premise that because language neither corresponds to reality nor represents it, because "words take their meanings from other words . . . and vocabularies acquire their privileges from the [people] who use them," knowledge is fluid and must be defined in the agreements of people bound together by their shared circumstances (368). What we say we know is what we can agree upon within the communities we have built upon a "hope for agreement," communities where conversation, a process in which disagreements are continually "compromised or transcended," is the primary activity through which that hope is sustained (317–18). Coming to know, for Rorty, is like "getting acquainted": it is a process in which we "play back and forth between guesses about how to characterize particular statements or other events, and guesses about the point of the whole situation, until gradually we feel at ease with what was hitherto strange" (319). Consequently, our most essential knowledge is "the practical wisdom necessary to participate in a conversation" (372) that is the process of testing and justifying our beliefs within a particular community at a particular time, this because conversation is "the ultimate context within which knowledge is to be understood" (389).

When we understand discourse as an activity in which we participate with others in the ongoing process of constructing the knowledge that binds us together as a community and supports our collective action, we recognize that written discourse must likewise function within such a collaborative social context. And that recognition necessarily extends our rhetorical awareness when we write or read beyond the components of any immediate rhetorical situation—beyond a particular exigence, audience, and set of constraints—to the larger historical conversation in which that situation has function and meaning. Walter Ong notes in *Orality and Literacy* that the function of writing in human communities is both "intersubjective"—the knowledge it expresses is shaped by one person who has another "in mind" as the writer adapts both knowledge and self to the anticipated response of a reader (176–77)—and "intertextual"—each text is developed in response and in reference to a "tradition" of texts that has preceded it (133). It is only within the context of such a tradition that writing can be read, that it can invoke a community of readers who will read a text in a way that can contribute to the making of shared meaning.[15]

If we recognize that what we write must function within the context of such a historical conversation in which some aspect of the shared knowledge that sustains a community is being constructed, we can understand better what we must teach when we teach people to write. For example, we can understand what Bitzer meant when he described effective discourse as rhetoric "fitting" in its situation. Writing that "fits" in a conversation must be informed by the state of shared knowledge—knowledge of both matters at issue and conventions of addressing them—as it has been defined in the past, if it is to contribute constructively. Further, because the conversation model allows us to understand that writing is, at some level, always an exertion of power over others, it reminds us that we must write and read texts with responsibility and care. If, as Bitzer observes, rhetoric allows us to alter "reality by bringing into existence a discourse of such a character that the audience, in thought and action, is so engaged that it becomes a mediator for change" (1968, 4), then rhetoric that is written has even more power to engage an audience to alter reality because texts continue to address audiences over time, audiences who continue to respond in ways that can amplify the effect of a text on the direction of a conversation.

The conversation model for the social function of writing makes us aware that when we write or read we join an ongoing social exchange, and that what we write or read is thus necessarily connected to what others have written and read before. It makes us aware that every text is situated within the context of a conversation in which it presents and justifies an interpretation of common experience that its writer believes a community should share. In doing so, it reminds us that writing is, in some sense, almost always public discourse in this attempt to contribute to the shared knowledge upon which the people whom a community comprises construct their collective life. When we recognize that texts function as a part of the historical conversation through which people continually redefine their commonality and thus their reality, we can begin to understand that every text, whether it is one we write or read, is almost always the attempt of one person to suggest to others what they can together believe and do.

4

Sustaining Conversation: The Ethics of Reading

DIALOGUE, DIALECTIC, AND CONVERSATION—THE THEORETICAL perspectives on the social function of writing that have come to dominate the disciplines that converge in composition studies—are brought to convergence themselves in Richard Weaver's fundamental observation that the language we use is inherently and inevitably "sermonic." In Weaver's classic statement: "We are all of us preachers in private or public capacities. We have no sooner uttered words than we have given impulse to other people to look at the world, or some part of it, in our way. Thus caught up in a great web of inter-communication and inter-influence, we speak as rhetoricians affecting one another for good or ill" (178). What rhetoric represents, for Weaver, is an attempt by one person to define for others a truth they all will share, a claim to power that is the private purpose that propels much of what we say to others and, particularly, most of what we write. Dialogue, dialectic, and conversation all describe social interactions through which those private purposes are made public and are publicly mediated, in a process of exchange in which the beliefs and values that bind people together as a community in knowledge and action are continually negotiated. If the members of a community do not actively sustain these interactions, they risk allowing the discourse that addresses them to define their beliefs and values for them, to stand among them as unmediated assertions of power.

That is the primary lesson these separate but similar notions of dialogue, dialectic, and conversation have to teach us, a lesson I will explore in this chapter by examining the ethics for writing and reading that they imply, and in the next chapter by describing the perspective on the teaching of writing and reading they suggest. Because I believe the ethical and pedagogical consequences of all three notions are essentially the same, I will treat them as one in these two chapters, calling them by the name that has provided scholars in disciplines ranging from composition to philosophy with a vigorous explanatory metaphor for the social function of discourse: conversation.

If a written text finds its public function within a process of collaborative exchange in which writer and readers negotiate beliefs they can share, it is not because such negotiation was the writer's purpose. Implicitly or explicitly, writers write for the purpose of inducing others to adopt their beliefs. And because we cannot *not* fully believe what it is we believe, nor, when we express those beliefs, *not* try to persuade others to accept them, that purpose is unavoidable.[1] That is Weaver's point. Our private purpose when we write is not to provide grist for the mill of public deliberation, but to persuade others to believe what we believe. It is a purpose that, if realized, would preempt any collaborative function our written statements might have, yet that purpose is inherent in the very nature of rhetoric.

Classically, rhetoric functions within a community to establish the shared knowledge, the commonly held values and beliefs Thomas B. Farrell calls "social knowledge" ("Knowledge, Consensus, and Rhetorical Theory" 5), that binds its members together and allows them to coordinate their collective actions. This is the function Aristotle emphasized in his discussion of the enthymeme as a statement that extends shared knowledge in a direction that the person who states it believes the audience will probably accept. Aristotle emphasizes, however, that in order to provide an audience with a concrete object for judgment such statements must present that proposed extension as if the audience had already accepted it, as if it had already been authorized by their assent. With that presentation the work of rhetoric is complete and the audience is left with the responsibility to judge for themselves.[2] This tendency of rhetoric—to present what is only someone's belief by portraying that belief as if it carried the authority of shared, social knowledge—

creates the ethical problems that have always been rhetoric's burden. By presenting our beliefs to others as if they had already judged and accepted them we not only assume their assent, we demand it. And when our statement is written rather than spoken, both that assumption and its implicit demand are intensified because, as readers from Plato to Derrida have noted, written texts present themselves as independent of the people who wrote them: as immutable and ultimately unassailable. Inherent in rhetoric, then, and particularly in written rhetoric, is one person's claim to the authority to determine what others can together believe and do. If the people whom rhetoric addresses do not actively challenge such claims with the critical judgment that results in an assertive response, they risk allowing the knowledge that constitutes them as a community to become an aggregate of those beliefs that have been most effectively imposed.

Farrell's explanation of the means through which rhetoric establishes knowledge within a community describes the process whereby this can happen. The kind of agreement that validates what he calls social knowledge is created and extended by rhetorical statements that "attribute" to the community they address a consensus that does not yet exist, a consensus that members of that community can bring into existence only when they confirm its function as shared, social knowledge among them by acting upon it (8–9). Consequently, rhetorical statements that attribute to an audience beliefs they do not yet hold in a way that not only invites but almost compels their acknowledgment have the power, in Farrell's words, to "generate what they can initially only assume" (11). And this power is intensified when the rhetoric is written. A writer writes as a speaker speaks, proclaiming the consensus that would transform a private belief into public knowledge. Unlike the statements of a speaker, however, whose accessibility can remind an audience that the speaker is in some way one of them and therefore allows if not invites their critical response, written texts assert their private purposes seemingly unchallenged. Yet if those purposes are not challenged the consensus that results, and the knowledge it authorizes, will be, in a sense, coerced.

If the consensus that contributes to the definition and direction of a community is to be the product of collaboration rather than of coercion, the written texts that address that community, like spoken statements, must be submitted to the very process of critical exchange that it is their nature to resist. This means, I believe, that those who read texts rather than those who write them must carry the primary responsibility for seeing that writing functions ethically—which means cooperatively and collaboratively—within a community.[3] If readers are to do that, they must adopt an alternative notion of the consensus that members of a community seek, a consensus in which the agreement they try to establish is not one that would eliminate conflict among them, but one that would structure the process that enables them continually to confront it.

Consensus, Private Purposes, and the Elimination of Conflict

What binds a community of people together in shared knowledge and collective action is a hierarchy of consensual values that is continually subjected to revision in what Wayne Booth calls the "courts of communal exchange" (148). Consequently, we use rhetorical statements within such communities to assert the primacy of particular values—essentially an alternative hierarchy—that will support what we believe to be proper collective actions.[4] And because values can be validated only by the consent of those who are to share them, our purpose in making such assertions is to establish within that community a consensus that will confirm the primacy of the values we present. We attempt to establish that consensus through a rhetorical presentation that portrays those values as if the community we address had already confirmed them, as if they were already consensual. Although the values our rhetoric asserts are likely to be in some form already tacitly accepted within that community, our assertion of their primacy constitutes an attempt to effect change because the community's consent to that primacy will subordinate other values and carry collective actions in a new direction.

Aristotle described such statements that assert the priority of particular values already held but not necessarily enacted in his discussion of the epideictic function of rhetorical discourse. Unlike deliberative and legal discourse that address directly what members of a community should consider preferable action, epideictic discourse addresses the nature of the preferable itself for the purpose of establishing within that community a consensus that will validate the values upon which particular collective actions would be based (32–33) and intensifying the community's commitment to them (56–58). And it is in this epideictic purpose that Chaim Perelman has found a description of the purpose he argues must propel every rhetorical statement: to establish "a consensus in the minds of the audience regarding the values that are celebrated in the speech" ("The New Rhetoric" 6). Because every rhetorical statement attempts to establish the kind of consensus that confirms the values that would support the collective action it seeks, argues Perelman, all rhetoric is essentially epideictic in its social function (*The Realm of Rhetoric* 20). Like statements that are explicitly epideictic, all rhetorical statements present the values they assert as inherently correct, inviting those they address to acknowledge that correctness rather than judge it, to be witnesses to the inherent validity of those values rather than collaborators in the process of determining their validity.[5] This suggests that rhetorical statements are inherently more "performative" than "propositional," that a rhetorical presentation is more an attempt to impose a particular value structure on its audience than an invitation to them to collaborate in the process of constructing one.[6] And that suggests that our purpose in using rhetoric is to impose upon others a version of shared, social knowledge that is, inevitably, ideological.

Rhetorical statements are assertions of ideology because their claim to consensus presents particular preferences as if they were absolute principles. Our rhetoric does that because we each perceive our particular preferences as inherently correct, expressing as they do that "whole system of thought and belief" about the social world that "structure[s] our thinking so deeply that we take them for granted, as the nature of the real world"—Greg Myers's definition of ideology (156). Every rhetorical statement we make necessarily applies the private social ideal that not only defines our own values but also determines our own perception of reality itself to the particular social circumstances we address. That is why rhetoric must present preferences as if they were consensual: from the perspective of the people who make them, those statements state the truth and truth compels the consent of reasonable people. It is in this claim to truth that ideologies demand complete agreement.

And it is this demand for ideological consensus that defines for every rhetorical statement its practical purpose: to eliminate among those it addresses the possibility of conflict.

That is why ideology is at the root of the ethical problems that rhetoric presents. Because the reality it attempts to define is a social one, the ideology that every rhetorical statement must express makes that statement a claim to correctness, and thus to power within a community that is inevitably constituted of multiple ideologies coexisting in a state of competition, each claiming the consensus that would authorize and establish the particular social structure it envisions.[7] This makes rhetoric primarily defensive in purpose: we use it to defend the correctness of our social vision against the competing notions that coexist in the pluralistic community in which our statements must function. It is a purpose that puts us in a position that Perelman and Olbrechts-Tyteca describe as very much like "the guardian of dikes under constant assault by the ocean" (55). The purpose of any rhetorical statement, then, is to take the knowledge of those addressed in an ideological direction that will effectively limit or eliminate alternatives. In other words, we use rhetoric to impose upon others the ideology that is our reality by attempting to establish it among them by a consensus characterized by nothing less than complete agreement. And although achieving such an absolute consensus is, in practice, almost impossible, that is what every rhetorical statement attempts to establish by claiming that consensus already exists.

An attempt to establish this kind of consensus within a community is essentially coercive because it requires that alternative beliefs, values, or actions be considered inherently incorrect, denying the possibility of conflict by situating rhetorical exchange in a closed context where disagreements are either suppressed or ignored. Indeed, the rhetorical assertion of such a consensus represents an attempt to confine the possibilities for discursive exchange in that community within a set of ideological assumptions that the rhetoric presents as absolute constraints imposed by the boundaries of reality. This results in what W. Lance Bennett describes as "systematic negation" (270), the largely unconscious tendency of those who make rhetorical statements to dismiss the possibility of alternative beliefs and actions, a process that he argues makes every rhetorical statement more an attempt at "impression management" than participation in a "critical dialogue" (268). It makes rhetoric an attempt to channel the community it addresses toward what he calls a "defective consensus" that will establish particular ideological claims as shared, social knowledge by eliminating conflicts and thus the possibility of significant challenge (264). That is why rhetoric demands nothing less than agreement on a single set of beliefs and values to be expressed in the collective actions of a community, actions that are self-evidently correct. From the perspective of rhetorical purpose, such a consensus creates the best of both worlds: with conflict eliminated in a process of exchange that admits only expressions of the particular ideology that the rhetoric asserts, the interaction that results creates, Bennett argues, "the positive illusion of dialogue, while negating the very possibility of dialectical transformation . . . that gives dialogue its traditional meaning" (271).

This private purpose that propels rhetorical statements is essentially authoritarian in its attempt to establish a state of consensus that would invalidate conflicting ideas and deny the diversity of experience and interpretation that characterizes any community. It is authoritarian in its claim to speak *for* the community it addresses as it displays to them a consensus it treats as already established. In Bakhtin's description, every such statement

> demands that we acknowledge it, that we make it our own; it binds us, quite independent of any power it might have to persuade us internally; we encounter it with its authority already fused to it. The authoritative word is located in a distanced zone, organically connected with a past that is felt to be hierarchically higher. It is, so to speak, the word of the fathers. Its authority was already *acknowledged* in the past. It is a *prior* discourse. ("Discourse in the Novel" 342)

Such statements function as "a compact and indivisible mass" that constitutes a claim to power that people in the community it addresses must "either affirm . . . or totally reject" (343). Those who affirm it subject themselves to its authority; those who reject it embody the conflict that statement denies. And when conflicts are denied, the rhetoric that sustains a community becomes necessarily, according to Bennett, "repressive, divisive, subversive to collective action and costly in terms of human potential" (260).

This is rhetoric's ethical problem. As it is the nature of rhetoric to assert a truth that is authorized by the particular ideology of the person who presents it, it is the nature of the community that statement addresses to be constituted of multiple ideologies that must coexist in conflict. Believing in the truth of what we say, we use rhetoric in an attempt to bring that community to an ideological consensus. But because of the impossibility of the kind of agreement our statements both assume and demand, that attempt actually contributes to a state of conflict our statements can neither acknowledge nor address. Because it is the nature of consensus to deny the ideological nature of knowledge and thus the validity of conflict, any attempt to establish such a consensus constitutes an attempt to establish what Perelman calls an "orthodoxy" that will officially ignore and consequently suppress difference and dissent. When that happens, constructive conversation can no longer occur and matters of collective knowledge and action must be decided in other kinds of interaction, interactions that Perelman suggests will push language aside in favor of "an armed struggle for power" ("Authority, Ideology, and Violence" 144–45).

Consensus and the Public Function of Conflict

Because our communities always comprise people who are guided by competing ideologies, any attempt to contain in an ideological consensus the beliefs and values that constitute a community requires some systematic denial and suppression of disagreement and dissent. Consequently, a community that is collaboratively constituted cannot maintain that kind of consensus. The problem is that the rhetorical statements we use to construct our communities are inevitably propelled by private purposes that demand that consensus by attempting to establish publicly the correctness of our beliefs in order to deny the validity of beliefs that differ.[8] Because rhetoric must, at some level, claim that kind of authority, the solution to that problem must become the responsibility of those to whom rhetoric is addressed, people who must learn to resist such claims by becoming what Perelman calls "proficient in pluralism" ("The Philosophy of Pluralism and the New Rhetoric" 71).

Although no rhetorical statement can be pluralistic in its purpose, the people it addresses can make it pluralistic and thus public in the way that it functions within their community. The person who asserts a rhetorical statement does so from within an ideological vision

that designates that statement as correct, but the people that statement addresses bring to their judgment of it alternative visions, and
they can respond to it with opposing statements of their own that
will enact the conflicts in ideology that constitute the community
they share. In doing so, they expose that rhetorical statement as an
assertion of an ideology, judge it as such, and present in response
alternative ideological claims for public consideration. Such responses exploit rather than deny the conflicts that exist within a
community, engaging the elements of that conflict itself in the public process of exchange in which commonalities and differences
within a community can be thoroughly examined and explored.[9]
Such pluralism may make community life a disorderly project, but
it provides a far more constructive opportunity for defining shared
knowledge and deciding collective actions than the alternative. In
Perelman's terms:

> Pluralism demands a search for moderate, and thus well-balanced solu-
> tions to all conflicts, which it considers nevertheless as unavoidable and
> recurring. Under the sign of reasonableness, pluralism does not claim
> to provide the perfect, unique and final solution, but simply human
> solutions—acceptable but capable of being changed and improved—to
> the ever-recurring problems created by the coexistence of [individuals]
> and groups, who prefer a fair compromise to the coercion imposed in
> the name of a unique value, irrespective of how important or even pre-
> eminent that value may be. ("The Philosophy of Pluralism" 71)

A community that is proficient in pluralism is constituted on the
basis of a very different kind of consensus than the authoritarian
consensus that would reconstruct a community in the ideological
image of the person whose rhetoric promotes it. Pluralism requires
that conflicting notions of shared, social knowledge coexist, and that
the conflicts themselves be publically explored. Consequently, it
necessitates that the conversations that sustain a community pro-
ceed not toward agreements that would end the exchange but toward the exposure of disagreements. In essence, it means that the
primary agreement that supports the process of conversation is the
agreement to converse. From this perspective, the consensus upon
which every conversation is built and toward which every conversation progresses is not so much an ideological agreement as it is an

agreement to continue to discuss ideologies, a consensus that brings people together not in their agreement on values and beliefs, but in their agreement to examine them (Farrell, "Knowledge" 6). From this perspective, shared, social knowledge is never fixed and made orthodox; it is continually discussed as the conflicts that emerge in that discussion are continually explored. That is because the process of conversation that sustains every community is necessarily fueled by conflict.

This pluralistic notion of consensus provides a foundation for the constructive function of a conversation that actually undermines the private purpose of rhetorical statements by compelling them to function publicly in the kind of critical exchange that exploits the conflicts that exist within every cooperating community. These conflicts, when exposed to public discussion, enable members of that community to extend the shared beliefs and values that constitute their social knowledge and, thus, enlarge the scope of their cooperation. In Bennett's terms, "the discovery of common concerns within competing realities is a point of departure for the transformation of conflict" (285), a statement that suggests that sustaining a process of inclusion rather than exclusion is the primary function of almost every linguistic exchange. This is the point of Kenneth Burke's vision of the unifying function of our communication: "Encountering some division, we retreat to a level of terms that allow for some kind of merger (as 'near' and 'far' are merged into the concept of 'distance') (A Grammar of Motives 440), a process that provides for us the "higher synthesis" through which we can accept the contradictions with which we, as members of communities, must live (Attitudes Toward History 92). Indeed, Bennett makes this process the centerpiece of his "code for socially responsible communication" that emphasizes that "opposing and mutually exclusive representations of the same thing should not be left as end states of communication" but should, instead, be "transformed into new symbolic terms that admit new experiences and actions into ongoing social relationships" (284).[10]

It is the public function of rhetoric to propel that process of transformation within a community of people who consent to the collaborative confrontation and exploration of conflict. Such a consensus must itself be understood as a process, one that requires that writers and readers continually redefine together the changing common ground upon which they can continue to converse. This is the kind of consensus that actually binds us together in communities and defines our social knowledge: our common consent to continue a particular conversation. And although that conversation must be based upon a collection of shared assumptions, they are temporary rather than fixed because they, too, are subject to examination and evaluation when, in the process of conversation, they are brought into conflict with other, alternative views. Writers who understand this know that when they write they release their convictions to the critical judgment of readers who do not necessarily share them. But understanding that doesn't lessen the intensity of a writer's claim to truth nor of the attribution of consensus that a writer's text presents to its readers. Even the most ethical of writers who *wants* her ideas to be read as contingent, who *seeks* from her readers their critical response, cannot prevent them from reading her text as a statement of consensual truth. It remains the responsibility of those who read even those texts to sustain the process of conversation. Only they can decide to read critically and to respond actively, and to enact as they do so the conversation process that enables written texts to function among them as contributions to the collaborative exchange that makes writer and readers equal partners in the continuous process of redefining their commonality.

Consensus and Authority in Conversation

Although every rhetorical statement is essentially a claim to power in which one person attempts to determine for others what they will together believe and do, such claims, regardless of the strength with which they are made, have no authority until the people whose beliefs and actions they address respond with their consent. Indeed, the ethical problem inherent in every rhetorical statement is situated in the moment that separates its claim to power from that subsequent authorizing consent. At the time of statement that claim is unauthorized and therefore false; what is claimed is transformed into something real only when it is actualized in the authorizing response of the people it addresses. The ethical function of rhetoric, then, must be understood in terms of this relationship between power and authority in a community.

According to Perelman, the words *power* and *authority* are not interchangeable: authority "authorizes," whereas power "enables," and the fundamental distinction that separates the two is consent. In a community where political equality is a founding principle, the only assertions of power that are ethical are those authorized by the people that power will affect ("Authority, Ideology, and Violence" 138). "To exercise power" in such communities, writes Perelman, "it is essential that it be recognized as legitimate and that it enjoy an authority that brings about the consent of those who are subject to it" (143). In Bitzer's terms, a rhetorical statement claims the power within a community to represent its members, to speak for them, but it is necessarily invalid until the self-proclaimed representative who made the statement is acknowledged and authorized by the consent of those she claims to represent ("Rhetoric and Public Knowledge" 73–77). This authorizing consent is given or denied through what Bitzer describes as a "testing" process that consists of "successive and overlapping rhetorical situations" in which statements that propose "public knowledge" may be "accredited" or "discredited and either abandoned or revised" (90).[11] That collaborative testing process is what I use the term *conversation* to describe.

Historically, the notion of conversation has had as much relation to people's living together as talking together. According to the *Oxford English Dictionary*, the word *conversation* has been understood to describe a manner of social conduct, as "having one's being in a place or among persons," as much as it has been understood to describe a manner of communication. Indeed, in articulating his contemporary ethics, Alisdair MacIntyre uses the term *conversation* to describe "the form of human transactions in general." Conversation is, for him, "a dramatic work . . . in which participants are not only the actors, but also the joint authors, working out in agreement or disagreement the mode of their production" (211). And *virtue,* or ethical action, MacIntyre argues, must necessarily be situated there. For him, "the . . . grounds for the authority of laws and virtues, can only be discovered by entering into those relationships which constitute communities whose central bond is a shared vision and understanding of goods." Consequently, ethical action consists of contributing to the kind of collaborative, progressing project in which individuals seek together the collective good of their community, a project that the notion of conversation, "understood widely enough," describes. Indeed, MacIntyre continues, "To cut oneself off from shared activity . . . , to isolate oneself from the communities which find their point and purpose in such activities, will be to debar oneself from finding any good outside of oneself" (258).

And that, I am arguing, is precisely what it is the nature of rhetorical statements to do. Although made in response to the conversation of a community, every rhetorical statement necessarily claims independence from that process when it portrays one person's preferred version of the knowledge shared by the people it addresses as a truth that is already authorized by their consent. In essence, the private purpose of every rhetorical statement is to isolate itself from the collaborative activity that it is the public function of rhetoric to sustain. Because ethical social action in a community of equals not only demands collaboration but is collaboration, rhetoric cannot function ethically within a community until it is subjected to the authorizing process of critical evaluation and exchange that the conversation model describes. This means that the writing of a text is an inherently unethical act that can be made ethical only through the judgment and response of those readers whose common interests it addresses. Without that, the ideological consensus that text attributes to that community will stand unexamined as a claim to power that its members have, indeed, authorized, even if by the default of their uncritical assent. Only readers who examine texts critically and respond to them responsibly can sustain within a community the kind of consensus that, in turn, sustains conversation there by exposing and exploring ideological conflicts in a process that treats knowledge as the object of discussion. That kind of consensus is constructive rather than destructive of communities, enabling those who compose them to cooperate in the process of authorizing what they will value and believe, and thus do, together.

As the great readers who preceded us have continually warned, written words have a power that makes reading a very risky thing. But because it is in the reading and not the writing that words are turned into action, readers and not writers can empower those words with the authority that allows them to function in the world. Without that authority, written words constitute nothing more than empty claims. What that suggests is that it is as readers even more than as writers that we can work for the common good. And that, I believe, is what Adrienne Rich meant in her fearful poem about the tenuous inadequacy of our communication, a poem she began with the statement, "A conversation begins with a lie" and ended with the admission that, for all the trouble, she must continue to participate in these "conversations/from which time after time the truth breaks moist and green."

5

Writing in Conversation and the Rhetoric of Democratic Education

To SAY THAT THE TEXTS WE WRITE FUNCTION IN INTERACTION with other texts to sustain a process of discursive exchange that resembles conversation, and to say that the function of this conversational exchange is to define and refine the shared knowledge that allows us to act cooperatively within a community, is to assert that the people who participate in that process are political equals who collaborate through their writing in the ongoing project of self-government. In other words, to adopt this model of the social function of writing is to adopt a political vision that is fundamentally democratic. But because self-government is so easily eroded, because the right to define shared knowledge and decide common action is so readily claimed by the few who come to dominate the discourse, real democracy can be maintained in a community only if all of its citizens participate actively in the ongoing process of directing their collective life. And because such participation requires of them both skill in expression and judgment in response, the survival of democracy in any community depends upon the education of its citizens. An education that sustains collaboration in a community will nurture in its citizens the skills and the judgment that enable them to participate constructively in these political conversations, skills and judgment they develop through the practice of rhetoric. That is why rhetoric must be placed at the center of a democratic education.[1]

Education in America was once democratic in this sense, and rhetoric was once at its center but is no longer. S. Michael Halloran has traced the history of our journey from there—where "a rhetoric of citizenship" was the unifying center of the American college curriculum (263)—to here—where the application of rhetoric that we call composition is, at best, but one requirement in an education that is essentially vocational. That journey began in a time in America when "public life was the great topic of both learning and discourse" and a student's education was constituted of speech and writing that "dealt importantly with public problems" before an audience that students could address as "fellow members of a commonwealth" ("Rhetoric in the American College Curriculum" 255–57). It was a time when the rhetoric of public discourse provided both the means and the ends of a democratic education. Since then, however, the topics of learning and discourse in the academy have narrowed to the disciplinary and, thus, the professional. And with that narrowing the rhetoric of public discourse has been replaced by a rhetoric of personal competence that enables our students only to advance their careers. That narrowing is illustrated in the continued prevalence in the composition classroom of individualistic assumptions about the function of writing. Whether the writer is taught to record a reality situated in the material world (the function of the rhetoric James Berlin describes as "objective") or to express the reality inherent in her own consciousness (the function of the rhetoric he describes as "subjective") (*Rhetoric and Reality* 6), these distinctions distinctly do not, in Halloran's words, "address students as political beings, as members of a body politic in which they have a responsibility to form judgments and influence the judgments of others on public issues" ("Rhetoric" 263).

But this, as Berlin suggests, seems to be changing.[2] As we who teach composition have begun in recent years to reexamine and revise the knowledge that guides our practice, we have been increasingly influenced by the dialogical/dialectical paradigms for the social function of discourse—particularly of written texts—that are coming to dominate the disciplines that we most frequently draw upon. Those paradigms have helped us understand that every written text functions socially as a part of an ongoing exchange of texts, an exchange that we have, for a decade now, been describing by the term *conversation*. And as this understanding of the social context of writing and the public function of written texts has come to dominate our discussions of what we do when we teach people to write, we have, I believe, begun to return to the recognition that writing is one way, and perhaps the most important way, that people participate in the self-government of their political, professional, and personal communities. In doing so, we have begun to return to the teaching of a rhetoric of democratic education. And although the explanatory work of our recent scholarship has begun that process, the perspective that work portrays is not often enacted in the practice of our teaching. My purpose in this final chapter is to assist us in enacting that rhetoric in our classrooms by extracting from the metaphor of conversation a rhetoric of public discourse that we can teach, a rhetoric that provides a perspective on the social function of texts that will enable us to reconceive the teaching of writing as the teaching of a democratic practice.

Assumptions

This rhetoric of public discourse is founded upon the assumption that much of human knowledge, particularly knowledge about shared values and the collective actions they support, is the product of negotiation; that our knowledge is socially constructed. According to that assumption, because knowledge must be constructed through the collaboration of people who share a common context of experiences and needs, the knowledge they construct is necessarily local and community-based. This understanding that we construct with our peers the knowledge we share in the exchange of our discourse necessitates the recognition that speech and writing are situated at the very center of our community life. In other words, once we assume that our knowledge is socially constructed, once we understand that we construct it in collaboration with our peers through the exchange of our discourse, we must recognize that, as Richard Rorty states, our "*conversation* [is] the ultimate context within which knowledge is to be understood" (*Philosophy and the Mirror of Nature* 389). This recognition that it is our own exchange of discourse rather than material reality or some transcendent authority that authorizes the shared knowledge that sustains our cooperation exposes our obligation as members of a community of cooperating people to participate in that conversation in a way that contributes to its quality. As Clifford Geertz asserts, once we recognize that "ours is but one voice among many and that, as it is the only one we have, we must needs speak with it," we can begin to understand why it is only through participation in the conversations that constitute the communities in which we live and act that we can "imagine principled lives [we] can practicably lead" (*Local Knowledge* 234).

This first assumption that our knowledge and thus our values and actions are the products of the provisional agreements that we negotiate and continually renegotiate in discourse with our peers leads to the second assumption that is its consequence: every statement that contributes to a conversation can present to a community, at best, only one person's interpretation, one person's preference, one person's argument. In other words, every claim to truth, situated as it is within an ongoing exchange in which it must function as a modifying response to the claims that have preceded it and a modifying influence on those that will follow, is inherently temporary and provisional. Indeed, such statements are nothing more and nothing less than what Stanley Fish describes as "political justifications" that recommend to a community "contrasting agendas for the frankly political consequences they would be likely to have" ("Consequences" 127). That is necessarily so because, given the first assumption that we establish the knowledge that guides us in the absence of what Fish calls "external and independent guides" that could confirm for us its absolute validity, the beliefs and values that direct our collective action must emerge from an open process of exchange in which the assertions of individuals are subjected to the judgment and modification of those whose interests they address.

Given these two fundamental assumptions about the nature and origin of shared knowledge, the community it defines can be understood to be inherently democratic as long as its members remain active participants in the constructive process of conversation. If participation is not full, however, that democracy will be limited or even eliminated as members of the community withdraw from that process and in doing so relinquish the right to construct and authorize the knowledge that directs them to those who continue to converse. In other words, democracy can be sustained only by the active participation of the members of a community in the process of judging every statement that addresses their common concerns and making those judgments public in response. And that participation must be sustained by a rhetoric of public discourse that enables members of a community, whether they function as speakers or audience, as writers or readers, to treat every word that is exchanged among them as, in Bakhtin's assessment, "directly, blatantly, oriented toward a future answer-word," a word that necessarily "provokes an answer, anticipates it and structures itself in the answer's direction" ("Discourse in the Novel" 280). Because this rhetoric describes participation in discourse as the particular kind of collaboration upon which the democracy of a community depends, the rhetoric of public discourse must hold the center of what one historian of the democratic education of Americans has described as "a publicly constitutive, personally liberating education" (Antczak 3–4).

This rhetoric of public discourse prescribes what Alasdair MacIntyre describes as a "practice," which he treats as the particular social context in which all socially constructive interaction, and thus all ethical action, must be situated. A "practice" is, in MacIntyre's analysis, a "socially established cooperative human activity" in which individual effort contributes not only to the individual progress of the practitioner but also to collective progress by contributing to the shared knowledge that guides practitioners in their work, and thus to the progress of the common practice itself (187). Because a practice is guided by rules and "standards of excellence" that are developed and revised by its practitioners over time, becoming practitioners necessitates that we "subordinat[e] ourselves within the practice in our relationship" to established practitioners (190–91). In that relationship of apprenticeship, we learn the rules that guide the practice, submit the products of our own practice to the judgment of others who apply those common standards, and, in the process, develop toward full collaboration as we progress to the point where our own practice contributes to the progress of the practice itself (194).

MacIntyre develops this discussion of a practice in an attempt to define an ethics that will resist the individualism that so readily fills the relativistic void that seems left when we accept the assumptions that our knowledge is socially constructed and that statements of truth cannot be rooted in some absolute, external authority. Individualism, according to MacIntyre, would fill that void with private preferences alone and would define community as nothing more than an "arena" for separate and autonomous enterprise, where shared knowledge would be limited to beliefs that would protect the right of individuals to determine the separate directions of their lives for themselves (195). Because this leads to nihilism at best and, at worst, to the anarchy that precedes tyranny, MacIntyre argues that our only alternative is to situate ourselves within a community where we can work with others to define the shared beliefs and values that will enable us to live and work together. This, ultimately, is what MacIntyre means by "practice"—cooperating with others in the process of developing and improving the knowledge that enables us to meet our common needs and reach our common goals. This notion of practice situates our individual action within the context of the common project that we work with others to sustain. We do this cooperative work largely through the process of rhetorical exchange.

Applications

When we teach our students that writing is a "practice," as MacIntyre uses the term, we are teaching them reading and writing as a democratic practice, one sustained by the skills and judgment that a rhetoric of public discourse provides. That, I am asserting in this study, is what the notions of dialogue, dialectic, and conversation present to people who teach writing. These notions demonstrate that the exchange of discourse is the fundamental form of democratic practice. And that, I am arguing, is what we should teach when we teach writing. We should teach our students that every text—whether written or read—is necessarily suspended in an exchange of texts in which it contributes to the collaborative process through which the knowledge that constitutes the community that comprises its writer and readers is continually reconstructed. We should teach our students that the texts they write and read can have meaning only within the context of that process, and that those texts make the meaning they have by modifying a state of shared knowledge. Consequently, our students should learn from us that neither writing nor reading can be a private act, that every text is necessarily public and political as it contributes to the perpetual process in which the values and beliefs that sustain community life are modified and revised, that writing and reading are both public acts that carry with them significant social responsibility.

If we are to teach writing as a democratic practice we must begin by teaching our students to read. "To enter into a practice," writes MacIntyre, "is to enter into a relationship not only with its contemporary practitioners, but also with those who have preceded us in the practice, particularly those whose achievements extended the reach of the practice to its present point" (194). When the practice they need to enter is, as it usually is, constituted at least partially in the exchange of discourse, we need to teach our students that they cannot contribute responsibly to that exchange until they understand both the current state of shared knowledge in the community and the further needs common to its members, needs that the knowledge they share does not yet meet. Our students must learn that they can develop this understanding only by reading the texts that brought the practice of constructing that community to its current status; by, in other words, researching the history of the conversation of its practitioners. In doing this they act as apprentice practitioners who use reading to learn both the rules and the standards that, within this community, guide the practice of reading and writing texts in critical response. As they learn from this apprenticeship what constitutes constructive contributions to that conversation—contributions that might help that community meet its current needs—their relationship to the practitioners whose texts they have been reading changes from that of imitative apprentice to that of critical collaborator, and they begin to write texts that can contribute significantly and originally to the practice of sustaining the community.

There is nothing really new in this suggestion. This perspective on the teaching of writing and reading is inherent in our current notion that knowledge and discourse are both situated in the context of discourse communities, and, particularly, in the notion that we can best teach our students to write by teaching writing in the context of the particular academic discourse communities in which they must immediately function.[3] In doing so, Patricia Bizzell cautions, we should emphasize "the concept of discourse, the idea that language use in any social context is formed into a regular discourse by the collaborative efforts of the people who have worked and are working in the discourse," that, above all, "academic discourse"— or the discourse of any community—"is a changing practice that they have the chance of influencing even as it influences them"

("Foundationalism and Anti-Foundationalism in Composition Studies" 45). We need to teach our students that the particular academic, professional, or political communities in which they must work are, in fact, communities of practitioners bound together by the knowledge that guides their particular practice where the primary act of individual practice is participation in the exchange of discourse through which practitioners collaboratively revise that knowledge. When they learn that what they write as well as what they read functions within a particular community as "a form of social action" that engages others in "the negotiation of meaning" (Faigley and Hansen 148–49), they will recognize that they have the same responsibilities as writers and as readers: "to anchor a message to a discourse community" (163), as Freed and Broadhead put it, both to read and to write in the context of the understanding they have of the knowledge and the needs shared by its members.

This recognition of responsibility to a community of collaborating others provides the foundation upon which any democratic practice must be built. It provides the context within which we can teach our students that their writing and their reading that prompts it are together the democratic practice through which they participate in the process of sustaining the communities that provide them with what they know. As they come to understand that responsibility, they come to understand that they can never be isolated and autonomous in their knowledge because, as Bizzell has more recently written, "knowledge is not a content conveyed by rhetoric. Knowledge is what ensues when rhetoric is successful, when rhetoricians and audiences reach agreement. If this is true, the . . . rhetoricians cannot share a community's knowledge while remaining unchanged. Rhetoricians' own worldviews will be influenced to the extent that they assimilate the community's knowledge to their own discourse" ("Arguing about Literacy" 149). When our students understand that, they will understand the public function of their reading and their writing. They will understand, Geoffrey Chase indicates, that they write and they read "as a part of a larger project in which they can affirm their own voices, learn how to exercise the skills of critical interrogation, and, finally, exercise the courage to act in the interests of improving the quality of human life" (21–22). They will understand that their writing and reading are perhaps their primary acts of democratic practice.

Consequences

Although it is the tendency of every written text to claim its own correctness and completeness, it is the function of a rhetoric of democratic practice to reject that claim by subjecting every written text to public judgment and response. That keeps conversation going within a community, and conversation keeps a community alive. As Richard Rorty writes, "to look for commensuration rather than simply continued conversation—to look for a way of making further redescription unnecessary by finding a way of reducing all *possible* descriptions to one—is to attempt to escape from humanity" (*Philosophy and the Mirror of Nature* 376–77). And to adapt Rorty's recommendations to philosophers to us as teachers of writing and reading, keeping a conversation going is a sufficient aim of a writer who writes and a reader who reads within a community; it is a sufficient aim, that is, of writers and readers who see citizenship constituted in the ability to sustain a conversation (378). The ultimate consequence of adopting this perspective on the social function of writing is that the boundaries of a community are expanded as people extend their willingness to collaborate.

Kenneth Burke sees this consequence as essential for our time because it has the potential to provide us with a nonlethal method for managing conflict. A rhetoric of democratic practice enables people to accept each other as they bridge the gap that separates them in order to collaborate in defining the common ground upon which they can continue to build their sense of collectivity. As Burke explained in *Attitudes Toward History*, our social life constantly requires us to confront conflicts and act to resolve them. When we confront conflicts that seem unresolvable, we must nonetheless know how to erect that "higher synthesis" that will help us find resolution or at least accommodation (92), that process of community building he described so concisely as: "Encountering some division, we retreat to a level of terms that allow for some kind of merger (as 'near' and 'far' are merged into the concept of distance): then we 'return' to the division, now seeing it as pervaded by the spirit of the 'One' we had found in our retreat" (*A Grammar of Motives* 440). The consequence of this process, Burke argues, is nothing less than progress toward "the purification of war" that emerges as we recognize that we are necessarily members of a larger community, a community of people who must use discourse to collaborate in the practice of surviving.

S. Michael Halloran tells the story of a Vietnam veteran with the credentials to teach in the university yet who chooses to remain in a tough public school teaching reading and writing because, in his words, "I don't want people to kill each other" ("Letter from Camp"). His story illustrates the importance of teaching our students a rhetoric of public discourse, a rhetoric in which language is seen as public and, thus, political. And in a world where written language is becoming increasingly powerful in its ability to influence people, this story illustrates the importance of teaching our students that embedded in the acts of reading and writing are fundamental human interactions, interactions that determine the direction of our common experience.

Notes

Works Cited

Notes

1. Discourse in Dialogue: The Social Context of Writing

1. A dialogue sustained among scholars in rhetoric that has been important in the development of this perspective was begun in an article by Richard L. Johannesen: "The Emerging Concept of Communication as Dialogue," *Quarterly Journal of Speech* 57 (1971): 373–82. Roderick P. Hart and Don M. Burks responded to Johannesen in "Rhetorical Sensitivity and Social Interaction," *Speech Monographs* 39 (1971): 75–91, which was followed by John Stewart's "Foundations of Dialogic Communication," *Quarterly Journal of Speech* 64 (1978): 183–201, and Ronald C. Arnett's "Toward Phenomenological Dialogue," *Western Journal of Speech Communication* 45 (1981): 201–12.

2. People in composition studies have begun to discuss how the dialogical notion of communication provides a perspective on the study of texts that might bring their work, which examines how texts are written, closer to the work of people in literature studies, which examines how texts are read. Patricia Bizzell argues that the "insight . . . that human beings make meaning when they use language" has significant and similar implications for both scholarly communities because it provides the framework for a theory of writing and reading that might unify the research and pedagogy of both: "On the Possibility of a Unified Theory of Composition and Literature," *Rhetoric Review* 4 (1986): 174–79.

3. C. Jack Orr distinguishes between two views of what we mean when we say that reality is socially constructed: the "intersubjective" view that defines reality as constructed through communication, and what is not so constructed as not real or true; and the "critical rationalist" view that defines reality as "conceptually organized and interpreted" through communication, but the resulting construct as only a partial version of a reality or truth that is yet inaccessible. He argues that only

the second will preserve us from the danger of considering a construct to be absolute: "How Shall We Say: 'Reality Is Socially Constructed through Communication?'" *Central States Speech Journal* 29 (1978): 263–74.

4. A similar notion of the origin and function of shared knowledge within a community is developed by Lloyd Bitzer in his discussion of rhetoric as statements of "public knowledge": "Rhetoric and Public Knowledge," in *Rhetoric, Philosophy, and Literature: An Exploration*, ed. Don M. Burks (West Lafayette, Ind.: Purdue University Press, 1978), 67–93.

5. Two equally helpful but quite different introductions to Bakhtin's work are Tzvetan Todorov's *Mikhail Bakhtin: The Dialogical Principle*, trans. Wlad Godzich (Minneapolis: University of Minnesota Press, 1984), and Katerina Clark and Michael Holquist's *Mikhail Bakhtin* (Cambridge: Harvard University Press, 1984). Todorov presents a concise and conservative introduction to Bakhtin's thought as a theoretical system; Clark and Holquist provide a more detailed intellectual biography that discusses the development of his thought in the context of his history. Most of Bakhtin's books are available in translation, and many of his essays are now being collected and published. See the Todorov and the Clark and Holquist bibliographies.

6. This is the concept of writing that supports current discussion in both fields. Patricia Bizzell's article "On the Possibility of a Unified Theory of Composition and Literature," *Rhetoric Review* 4 (1986): 174–79, provides a brief overview of the compatible substance of both bodies of theory. Karen Burke LeFevre's Studies in Writing and Rhetoric monograph *Invention as a Social Act* (Carbondale: Southern Illinois University Press, 1987), as well as Sonja K. Foss, Karen A. Foss, and Robert Trapp's *Contemporary Perspectives on Rhetoric* (Prospect Heights, Ill.: Waveland Press, 1985), provide accessible introductions to this perspective in current rhetorical theory. Terry Eagleton's *Literary Theory: An Introduction* (Minneapolis: University of Minnesota Press, 1983) contributes a useful introduction to its role in current literary theory.

7. Bakhtin introduced his notion of answerability in his earliest work, which remains unfinished and unpublished, but it is reflected throughout all his subsequent work. See chap. 3, "The Architectonics of Answerability," (63–94), in Clark and Holquist's *Mikhail Bakhtin*.

8. *Marxism and the Philosophy of Language* (trans. Ladislav Matejka and I. R. Titunik [Cambridge: Harvard University Press, 1986]), first published in 1929, is one of the number of books and essays attributed to Bakhtin although published under the names of others. Because Bakhtin himself never acknowledged many of these, including *Marxism*, his

authorship remains unconfirmed. Whether *Marxism*, published under the name of V. N. Voloshinov, was written by Bakhtin alone, by some sort of collaboration of the two, or only under his influence has not been determined. Clark and Holquist argue in *Mikhail Bakhtin* that Bakhtin was the principal if not sole author, and they offer a detailed explanation of political constraints that would have prevented him from signing the work or acknowledging it later; Todorov, however, argues that *Marxism* may indeed be the work of Voloshinov. The question remains unsettled by the contradictory testimony of a number of eyewitnesses. I will follow Todorov in listing the book as written by "Bakhtin/Voloshinov," but Clark and Holquist (along with most of the people in English studies who use Bakhtin) in treating the book as Bakhtin's.

9. Walter Ong describes *intertextuality* as the natural process in which texts are derived in reference to other texts through borrowings and adaptations, a process that persists despite the myths of originality that dominate print culture (*Orality and Literacy: The Technologizing of the Word* [London: Methuen, 1982], 133). I use the term in a broader sense to describe not only the nature of the process of writing a text but also the process of reading one. Meaning is produced collaboratively in the interaction of the text the writer writes and the text the reader reads, texts that are not, given the distinction between utterance and understanding, the same.

10. Lisa Ede and Andrea Lunsford developed this distinction in their article "Audience Addressed/Audience Invoked: The Role of Audience in Composition Theory and Pedagogy," *College Composition and Communication* 35 (1984), 155–71.

11. Bialostosky ("Dialogics as an Art of Discourse in Literary Criticism," *PMLA* 101 [1986]: 788–96) opposes dialogics to the two traditional arts of discourse, rhetoric and dialectic, as one that will not suffer from their limitations: "I would say that dialectic aims at discovering the truth of ideas or theses, rhetoric at determining the decisions of people, the dialogics at articulating the meaning of people's ideas, our own and those of others" (789). I agree with his distinctions in general but must add that the three are not necessarily discrete, parallel entities. They are, instead, differing emphases that can be interwoven in discourse.

2. *Rhetoric in Dialectic: The Functional Context of Writing*

1. Perelman describes in this essay three kinds of dialogue: *eristic*, in which the purpose of discourse is to present a thesis that will defeat competing theses; *critical*, in which the purpose is to expose flaws in a

thesis that has been presented; and *dialectical,* in which the purpose is to find points of agreement between contending theses. In my discussion of *eristic discourse* I am conflating Perelman's eristic and critical purposes and opposing them to *dialectical discourse.*

2. Richard McKeon distinguishes the two by defining *dialogue* simply as an exchange of questions and answers, and *dialectic* as an "art of discourse" in which a dialogical exchange is directed toward the specific purpose of establishing truth ("Greek Dialectics: Dialectic and Rhetoric, Rhetoric and Dialogue," in *Dialectics,* ed. Chaim Perelman, 1–25 [The Hague: Martinus Nihjoff, 1975], 1). Perelman's distinction is similar, designating dialectic "a process of criticism" situated in a dialogue that progresses toward the demonstration of some kind of truth ("The Dialectical Method" 164).

3. George A. Kennedy's *Classical Rhetoric and Its Christian and Secular Tradition from Ancient to Modern Times* (Chapel Hill: University of North Carolina Press, 1980) divides the literature of rhetoric into three traditions: the technical, the sophistic, and the philosophical. Although my categories of eristic and dialectical rhetorics do not neatly mesh with Kennedy's system, the first addresses what Kennedy describes in the technical tradition, and the second addresses much of what he describes in the sophistic and philosophical traditions.

4. This is the conclusion reached by Jasper Neel in his *Plato, Derrida, and Writing* (Carbondale: Southern Illinois University Press, 1988). Neel concludes his deconstructive reading of what both Plato's *Phaedrus* and Derrida's discussion of it, "Plato's Pharmacy," have to say about the teaching of writing by asserting that students need to learn to write "strong discourse," a term Neel borrows from Gilbert Romeyer-Dherbey's discussion of the Sophists to describe texts that exist "in a cacophonous plurality of other voices." Neel continues: "Strong discourse never succeeds in silencing all its competitors, for no discourse can remain strong without being surrounded by competitors. . . . Implicit in the idea of strong discourse is the belief that wisdom consists in knowing how in persuasion and argumentation to replace personal discourse with global discourse by replacing a weak conception with a strong one" (208–9).

One of the most useful discussions of these social constructionist assumptions as inherent in classical rhetorical theory is John Gage's. He presents a thorough and accessible explication of this dialectical rhetoric in classical terms in his "An Adequate Epistemology for Composition: Classical and Modern Perspectives," in *Essays on Classical Rhetoric and Modern Discourse,* ed. Robert J. Connors, Lisa S. Ede, and Andrea A. Lunsford, 152–69 (Carbondale: Southern Illinois University Press, 1984).

5. This dialectical perspective on the composition process itself is examined in detail in Karen Burke LeFevre's *Invention as a Social Act* (Carbondale: Southern Illinois University Press, 1987).

6. This summary is indebted to Richard Weaver's "The *Phaedrus* and the Nature of Rhetoric," in his *The Ethics of Rhetoric* (Chicago: Henry Regnery Co., 1953).

7. Two useful discussions of this focus in the *Phaedrus* are Ronna Burger's *Plato's Phaedrus: A Defense of a Philosophical Art of Writing* (University: University of Alabama Press, 1980) and Jacques Derrida's "Plato's Pharmacy" in his *Dissemination*, trans. Barbara Johnson (Chicago: University of Chicago Press, 1981).

8. Chaim Perelman provides a concise summary of Aristotelian reasoning in the first chapter of *The Realm of Rhetoric*. Analytical reasoning is demonstrative, addressing matters that can be resolved absolutely through logic that establishes truth. By contrast, dialectical reasoning is argumentative, addressing matters that must be resolved in agreements because they cannot be resolved absolutely, and thus is a process of establishing not truth but justifiable opinion. Perelman designates as Aristotle's notion of dialectic this process of argument as sustained by a few individuals who can interact immediately, and as his notion of rhetoric that process when sustained by a larger community in which such immediate interaction is not possible (1–5).

9. Grimaldi (*Studies in the Philosophy of Aristotle's Rhetoric* [Wiesbaden: Franz Steiner Verlag GmbH, 1972]) suggests that the matters addressed by rhetoric—matters of practical knowledge and action relevant to public concern—make rhetoric broader in its application than dialectic, which is limited in Aristotle's definition to abstract and speculative matters of probability (56).

3. Writing in Conversation: The Conversation Model

1. These references to the conversation model are in Elaine Maimon, "Talking to Strangers," *College Composition and Communication* 30 (1979): 364–69; Charles Bazerman, "A Relationship Between Writing and Reading: The Conversational Model," *College English* 41 (1980): 656–61; and Kenneth Bruffee, "Collaborative Learning and the 'Conversation of Mankind,'" *College English* 46 (1984): 635–52.

2. The centrality of cooperation to conversation was emphasized by H. P. Grice in the "cooperative principle" that, in his description, consists of four maxims that describe the way contributions to a conversation must support the ongoing process: a speaker should tell the truth (quality), should tell the listeners what they need to know and no more (quan-

tity), should say what is relevant (relation), and should say it clearly (manner). See Grice's germinal essay, "Logic and Conversation," in *The Logic of Grammar*, ed. Donald Davidson and Gilbert Harman, 64–75 (Encino, Calif.: Dickenson Publishing Co., 1975). My description of Grice's maxims is adapted from Marga Kreckel, *Communicative Acts and Shared Knowledge in Natural Discourse* (London: Academic Press, 1981), 14.

3. To Kreckel, "shared knowledge" consists of the "social values" and the "social consensus" that have been negotiated in conversations in the past and that will be renegotiated in future conversations (18). Wayne A. Beach describes shared knowledge as "background under-standings" that consist of shared "cultural, relational, and linguistic knowledge" (199) as well as "spiritual, moral, and ethical commit-ments" (220) in "Background Understandings and the Situated Accom-plishment of Conversational Telling-Expansions," *Conversational Co-herence: Form, Structure, and Strategy,* ed. Robert T. Craig and Karen Tracy, 196–221 (Beverly Hills: Sage Publications, 1983).

4. Beach argues that participants in a conversation bring with them their "presuppositions" for the purpose of submitting them to a collaborative examination in which they will be revised and expanded. In this pro-cess, participants are "constantly involved in making sense of how oth-ers are making sense" (197). In her book *Conversation: How Talk Is Organized* (Beverly Hills: Sage Publications, 1984), Margaret L. Mc-Laughlin summarizes the consensus among researchers in conversation that the goal of the speaker in a conversation is to increase "the corre-spondence between what S knows, wants, and believes, and what H knows, wants, and believes" (41), a goal that suggests what Kenneth Burke describes as "identification."

5. Farrell describes shared knowledge with his own term, "social knowl-edge," which he developed in "Knowledge, Consensus, and Rhetorical Theory," *Quarterly Journal of Speech* 62 (1976): 1–14.

6. See Thomas S. Frentz, "Rhetorical Conversation, Time, and Moral Ac-tion" *Quarterly Journal of Speech* 71 (1985): 1–18, for a useful explo-ration of the natural rhetorical conversation. See Walter R. Fisher, "Narration as a Human Communication Paradigm: The Case of Public Moral Argument," *Communication Monographs* 51 (March 1984): 1–22, for a discussion of the assumptions that support the notion of rhetorical conversation.

7. My use of the term "public discourse" is based upon the description provided by S. Michael Halloran in "Rhetoric in the American College Curriculum: The Decline of Public Discourse," *PRE/TEXT* 3 (1982): 245–69. This concept is developed at length in Cicero's *De Oratore*

and is implicit in the works of both Plato and Aristotle as they discuss the use of rhetoric in the context of the public interest. However, I am using the term more broadly than either Halloran or these classical authors to describe discourse that supports any kind of collaborative collectivity, whether or not that collectivity is "official."

8. Dewey developed his notion of the public community in his *The Public and Its Problems* (Denver: Alan Swallow, 1927). Pierce described reality as the collective notions of particular communities of people that have no definite limits and are capable of extending that knowledge (see the discussion of Pierce in Elizabeth Flower and Murray G. Murphey, *A History of Philosophy in America* [New York: G. P. Putnam's Sons, 1977]). Thomas Kuhn's discussion of the function of scientific communities in *The Structure of Scientific Revolutions* (Chicago: University of Chicago Press, 1970) seems to build upon Pierce. In *The Problem of Christianity* (Chicago: University of Chicago Press, 1968), first published in 1917, Josiah Royce described "communities of interpretation" within which people exchange interpretations in the process of negotiating interpretations they can share (see chapter entitled "The Will to Interpret." 297–319). Stanley Fish's notion of "interpretive communities" as described in *Is There a Text in This Class?* (Cambridge: Harvard University Press, 1980) builds upon Royce. I am indebted to Grant Boswell for directing me to Pierce and Royce.

9. Bizzell has examined this issue in the following articles: "The Ethos of Academic Discourse," *College Composition and Communication* 29 (1978): 351–55; "Thomas Kuhn, Scientism, and English Studies," *College English* 40 (1979): 764–71; "College Composition: Initiation into the Academic Discourse Community," *Curriculum Inquiry* 12 (1982): 191–207; and "Cognition, Convention, and Certainty: What We Need to Know about Writing," *PRE/TEXT* 3 (1982): 213–43. For her more recent thinking see "Foundationalism and Anti-Foundationalism in Composition Studies," *PRE/TEXT* 7 (1986): 37–56; "What Happens When Basic Writers Come to College?" *College Composition and Communication* 37 (1986): 294–301; and "Arguing about Literacy," *College English* 50 (1988): 141–53.

10. In a paper presented at the 1986 meeting of the Conference on College Composition and Communication in New Orleans, "Academic Discourse: Taxonomy of Conventions or Collaborative Practice?" Bizzell distinguished two types of conversation within the conversation model: "conversation-as-dialogue," defined as face-to-face-conversation that is largely spontaneous and personal; and "conversation-as-discourse," defined as a written, or a more formal, statement made as a part of a rhetorical exchange that addresses the conflict that is created when the

current shared knowledge of a community is confronted with a proposal for its revision, a proposal that provides for that community an opportunity to judge (6).

11. "The Rhetorical Situation," *Philosophy and Rhetoric* 1 (1968): 1–14, and "Functional Communication: A Situational Perspective," in *Rhetoric in Transition: Studies in the Nature and Uses of Rhetoric*, ed. Eugene E. White, 21–38 (University Park: Pennsylvania State University Press, 1980).

12. Bitzer's two essays do suggest that rhetorical discourse functions within a larger context that is historical. He notes in the 1968 essay that rhetorical discourse belongs "to the class of things which obtain their character from the circumstances of the historical context in which they occur" (3), and in the 1980 essay that "the situation perspective considers thoughts as well as things to be parts of historic reality, and it calls attention to the close relation of pragmatic communication to actual historic conditions" (25).

13. For a more detailed description of conversation as a model for the social context in which rhetorical discourse functions see the chapter on historical conversation in Gregory Clark, "Timothy Dwight's *Travels in New England and New York* and the Rhetoric of Puritan Public Discourse," Diss. Rensselaer Polytechnic Institute, 1985.

14. This larger context, examined in terms of Bitzer's notion of rhetorical situation, is discussed in a number of theoretical studies. John H. Patton ("Causation and Creativity in Rhetorical Situations: Distinctions and Implications," *Quarterly Journal of Speech* 65 [1979]: 36–55) argues that, "the historical conditions of any situation must be included in any assessment of how and why rhetors define controlling exigencies and formulate purposeful discourse" (47). Patton observes that exigence, audience, and constraints cannot be defined by a rhetor in isolation, but "must be dialectically secured in the classical sense" (48). Robert L. Scott ("Intentionality in the Rhetorical Process," *Rhetoric in Transition: Studies in the Nature and Uses of Rhetoric*, ed. Eugene E. White, 39–60 [University Park: Pennsylvania State University Press, 1980]) notes that rhetorical discourse is composed and delivered "on a larger scene in which rhetoric is continuing. Into the larger context actors enter and exit . . . who may understand at any moment their situations as rhetorical and act accordingly" (57). Carolyn R. Miller ("Genre as Social Action," *Quarterly Journal of Speech* 70 [1984]: 151–67) emphasizes that rhetorical situations are "social constructs" that are defined in the process of ongoing exchange, and Eugene E. White ("Rhetoric as Historical Configuration," *Rhetoric in Transition: Studies in the Nature and Uses of Rhetoric*, 7–20) observes that be-

cause "all societal developments are continuations of that which is already in progress" (8), any exigence that can be defined is a current consequence of a historical process of "exigential flow" (15).

15. The notion of creating an audience was most significantly addressed by Ong in "The Writer's Audience Is Always a Fiction," *PMLA* 90 (1975): 9–21. It is examined more broadly by Lisa Ede and Andrea Lunsford in "Audience Addressed/Audience Invoked: The Role of Audience in Composition Theory and Pedagogy," *College Composition and Communication* 35 (1984): 155–171.

4. Sustaining Conversation: The Ethics of Reading

1. Stanley Fish has argued the inescapability of believing and attempting to persuade others to believe as we do in "Demonstration and Persuasion: Two Models of Critical Activity," in *Is There a Text in This Class?: The Authority of Interpretive Communities* (Cambridge: Harvard University Press, 1980) and, more recently, in "Consequences," in *Against Theory: Literary Studies and the New Pragmatism*, ed. W. J. T. Mitchell (Chicago: University of Chicago Press, 1985).

2. This is William M. A. Grimaldi's notion of the function of rhetoric that he bases on Aristotle's description of the enthymeme: "The art, or technique, of rhetoric is the ability to perceive and to present evidence which makes decision, and a definite decision, possible; but to stop with the presentation" (*Studies in the Philosophy of Aristotle's Rhetoric* [Wiesbaden: Franz Steiner Verlag GmbH, 1972], 27).

3. I presented an early version of this argument as "Communitarian and Authoritarian Functions of Rhetoric," a paper read at The Penn State Conference on Rhetoric and Composition in July, 1986, where I received responses that have been helpful as I have revised and developed it here.

4. This notion of the realm of rhetoric is implicit in the classical rhetorics of Plato, Aristotle, and Cicero and explicit in the contemporary rhetorics of Booth, Bitzer, Perelman, and Burke. See especially Chaim Perelman's essays "The New Rhetoric: A Theory of Practical Reasoning" (1–42) and "Authority, Ideology, and Violence" (139–45) in his *The New Rhetoric and the Humanities: Essays on Rhetoric and Its Applications* (Dordrecht, Holland: D. Reidel Publishing Company, 1979); and Bitzer's "Rhetoric and Public Knowledge," in *Rhetoric, Philosophy, and Literature: An Exploration*, ed. Don M. Burks, 131–55 (West Lafayette, Ind.: Purdue University Press, 1978).

5. This is the description of epideictic purpose developed in two impor-

tant contemporary studies of epideictic rhetoric, Bernard K. Duffy's "The Platonic Functions of Epideictic Rhetoric," *Philosophy and Rhetoric* 16 (1983): 79–83, and Lawrence W. Rosenfield's "The Practical Celebration of the Epideictic," *Rhetoric in Transition: Studies in the Nature and Uses of Rhetoric*, ed. Eugene E. White, 131–55 (University Park: Pennsylvania State University Press, 1980).

In an uncharacteristic lack of insight Kenneth Burke rehearses conventional wisdom by discussing Aristotle's notion of the epideictic as ceremonial discourse that addresses aesthetic rather than civic purposes. Describing it as a "catch-all" to cover what Aristotle's more useful descriptions of deliberative and legal rhetoric could not, Burke treats the epideictic as a genre that is most concerned with affirming the honor and virtue of the speech itself (*A Rhetoric of Motives* [Berkeley: University of California Press, 1969], 70–73). Wayne Booth's notion of the epideictic is more sophisticated; he describes it as the most prominent application of rhetoric in contemporary discourse but laments that state of things, worrying that the once-rational processes of collaborative decision making are being "overwhelmed by demonstrations for values" (*Modern Dogma and the Rhetoric of Assent* [Chicago: University of Chicago Press, 1974], 155).

6. Terry Eagleton used these terms in a paper titled "The Politics of Metaphor" that he read at the 1986 meeting of the Modern Language Association in New York City, December 27, 1986.

7. Beyond Myers's "Reality, Consensus, and Reform in the Rhetoric of Composition Teaching" (*College English* 48 [1986]: 154–74), Terry Eagleton's *Literary Theory: An Introduction* (Minneapolis: University of Minnesota Press, 1983) and Chaim Perelman's "Authority, Ideology, and Violence" provide excellent discussions of this ideological function of rhetorical discourse.

8. I am applying Stanley Fish's discussion of the ideological founding of theories in "Consequences" to this consideration of the ideological foundations of rhetoric. Fish argues that any theory is an inherently self-fulfilling structure that allows people to reach conclusions that seem absolutely valid but only because their theory expresses a particular set of ideologically based values and assumptions. I am arguing that the ideological system that is expressed by a rhetorical statement functions in much the same way.

9. Gerald Graff describes what he would like to see English departments become in just these terms—communities of people who exploit their ideological differences and the conflicts they create by making them the focus of their discussion, particularly within the classroom—in *Professing Literature: An Institutional History* (Chicago: University of Chicago Press, 1987).

10. This is Bennett's second of the three propositions of his code. This proposition suggests that the conversational notion of the social function of discourse is central to ethical communication. The first proposition ("Communicators should learn to avoid the use of social representations based on the systematic negation of other warrantable representations" [283]) and third ("Representations should be evaluated in regard to their capacities to accommodate facts or experiential claims that can be shown to be relevant to issues or values of comparable importance to all representations in the situation" [285]) describe the communication practices that must precede and follow this primary interaction.

11. Bitzer uses "public knowledge" to denote something similar to what I have been describing as the "shared, social knowledge" that binds people together as members of a community. Public knowledge, as Bitzer describes it, includes "principles of public life to which we submit as conditions of living together," shared goals and values as well as definitions and laws, and "the accumulated wisdom" of a common cultural history ("Rhetoric and Public Knowledge" 87).

5. Writing in Conversation and the Rhetoric of Democratic Education

1. Jasper Neel (*Plato, Derrida, and Writing* [Carbondale: Southern Illinois University Press, 1988]) makes essentially the same argument in the following terms: "Wouldn't the teaching of writing enable a democratic society by showing how to construct a position, how to deconstruct one, and how not to be fooled by those who claim to know truth, even if they make the claim by explaining that the truth of the truth is that no one knows it?" (99).

2. Recent work in the history of composition in America provides a variety of discussions of the changes in the teaching of writing, and many point to the possibility that we are returning to a less opportunistic, more rhetorically based pedagogy. See, for example, James Berlin's *Writing Instruction in Nineteenth-Century American Colleges* (Carbondale: Southern Illinois University Press, 1984) and *Rhetoric and Reality: Writing Instruction in American Colleges, 1900–1985* (Carbondale: Southern Illinois University Press, 1987), and Robert J. Connors's "Personal Writing Assignments," *College Composition and Communication* 38 (1987): 154–65.

3. David Bartholomae and Patricia Bizzell made fundamental statements that have directed the discussion of academic discourse communities as a focal point for the teaching of writing. See Bartholomae's "Inventing

the University" in *When a Writer Can't Write: Studies in Writer's Block and Other Composing-Process Problems,* ed. Mike Rose (New York: Guilford Press, 1985), 134–65, and Bizzell's "Cognition, Convention, and Certainty: What We Need to Know About Writing" in *PRE/ TEXT* 3 (1982): 213–43.

Works Cited

Antczak, Frederick J. *Thought and Character: The Rhetoric of Democratic Education*. Ames: Iowa State University Press, 1985.

Aristotle. *Rhetoric*. Trans. W. Rhys Roberts. *The Rhetoric and the Poetics of Aristotle*. New York: Modern Library, 1984.

Arnett, Ronald C. "Toward Phenomenological Dialogue." *Western Journal of Speech Communication* 45 (1981): 201–12.

Bakhtin, Mikhail. "Discourse in the Novel" (1935). *The Dialogic Imagination: Four Essays by M. M. Bakhtin*, ed. Michael Holquist, 259–422. Austin: University of Texas Press, 1981.

Bakhtin, Mikhail/V. N. Voloshinov. *Marxism and the Philosophy of Language* (1929). Trans. Ladislav Matejka and I. R. Titunik. Cambridge: Harvard University Press, 1986.

Barrett, Harold. *The Sophists: Rhetoric, Democracy, and Plato's Idea of Sophistry*. Novato, Calif.: Chandler and Sharp Publishers, 1987.

Bartholomae, David. "Inventing the University." *When a Writer Can't Write: Studies in Writer's Block and Composing-Process Problems*, ed. Mike Rose, 134–65. New York: Guilford Press, 1985.

Bazerman, Charles. "A Relationship between Writing and Reading: The Conversational Model." *College English* 41 (1980): 656–61.

Beach, Wayne A. "Background Understandings and the Situated Accomplishment of Conversational Telling-Expansions." *Conversational Coherence: Form, Structure, Strategy*, ed. Robert T. Craig and Karen Tracy, 196–221. Beverly Hills: Sage Publications, 1983.

Bennett, W. Lance. "Communication and Social Responsibility." *Quarterly Journal of Speech* 71 (1985): 259–88.

Berger, Peter L., and T. Luckman. *The Social Construction of Reality: A Treatise in the Sociology of Knowledge*. New York: Doubleday, 1966.

Berlin, James A. *Rhetoric and Reality: Writing Instruction in American Colleges, 1900–1985.* Carbondale: Southern Illinois University Press, 1987.

———. *Writing Instruction in Nineteenth-Century American Colleges.* Carbondale: Southern Illinois University Press, 1984.

Bialostosky, Don H. "Dialogics as an Art of Discourse in Literary Criticism." *PMLA* 101 (1986): 788–96.

Bitzer, Lloyd. "Functional Communication: A Situational Perspective." *Rhetoric in Transition: Studies in the Nature and Uses of Rhetoric,* ed. Eugene E. White, 21–38. University Park: Pennsylvania State University Press, 1980.

———. "The Rhetorical Situation." *Philosophy and Rhetoric* 1 (1968): 1–14.

———. "Rhetoric and Public Knowledge." *Rhetoric, Philosophy, and Literature: An Exploration,* ed. Don M. Burks, 67–93. West Lafayette, Ind.: Purdue University Press, 1978.

Bizzell, Patricia. "Academic Discourse: Taxonomy of Conventions or Collaborative Practice?" Conference on College Composition and Communication. New Orleans, 14 March 1986.

———. "Arguing about Literacy." *College English* 50 (1988): 141–53.

———. "Cognition, Convention, and Certainty: What We Need to Know about Writing." *PRE/TEXT* 3 (1982): 213–43.

———. "College Composition: Initiation into the Academic Discourse Community." *Curriculum Inquiry* 12 (1982): 191–207.

———. "The Ethos of Academic Discourse." *College Composition and Communication* 29 (1978): 351–55.

———. "Foundationalism and Anti-Foundationalism in Composition Studies." *PRE/TEXT* 7 (1986): 37–57.

———. "On the Possibility of a Unified Theory of Composition and Literature." *Rhetoric Review* 4 (1986): 174–79.

———. "Thomas Kuhn, Scientism, and English Studies." *College English* 40 (1979): 764–71.

———. "What Happens When Basic Writers Come to College?" *College Composition and Communication* 37 (1986): 294–301.

Booth, Wayne B. *Modern Dogma and the Rhetoric of Assent.* Chicago: University of Chicago Press, 1974.

Bruffee, Kenneth A. "Collaborative Learning and the 'Conversation of Mankind.'" *College English* 46 (1984): 635–52.

———. "Social Construction, Language, and the Authority of Knowledge: A Bibliographical Essay." *College English* 48 (1986): 773–90.

Buber, Martin. *Between Man and Man.* Trans. Ronald Gregor Smith. London: Routledge & Kegan Paul, 1947.

Burger, Ronna. *Plato's Phaedrus: A Defense of a Philosophical Art of Writing.* University: University of Alabama Press, 1980.

Burke, Kenneth. *Attitudes Toward History,* 3d ed. Berkeley: University of California Press, 1984.

———. *A Grammar of Motives.* Berkeley: University of California Press, 1969.

———. *The Philosophy of Literary Form: Studies in Symbolic Action,* 3d ed. Berkeley: University of California Press, 1973.

———. *A Rhetoric of Motives.* Berkeley: University of California Press, 1969.

Chase, Geoffrey. "Accommodation, Resistance, and the Politics of Student Writing." *College Composition and Communication* 39 (1988): 13–22.

Clark, Gregory. "Communitarian and Authoritarian Functions of Rhetoric." The Penn State Conference on Rhetoric and Composition. Pennsylvania State University, 8 July 1986.

———. "Timothy Dwight's *Travels in New England and New York* and the Rhetoric of Puritan Public Discourse." Diss. Rensselaer Polytechnic Institute. 1985.

Clark, Katerina, and Michael Holquist. *Mikhail Bakhtin.* Cambridge: Harvard University Press, 1984.

Connors, Robert J. "Personal Writing Assignments." *College Composition and Communication* 38 (1987): 154–65.

Derrida, Jacques. "Plato's Pharmacy." *Dissemination.* Trans. Barbara Johnson, 61–171. Chicago: University of Chicago Press, 1981.

Dewey, John. *The Public and Its Problems.* Denver: Alan Swallow, 1927.

Duffy, Bernard K. "The Platonic Functions of Epideictic Rhetoric." *Philosophy and Rhetoric* 16 (1983): 79–83.

Eagleton, Terry. *Literary Theory: An Introduction.* Minneapolis: University of Minnesota Press, 1983.

———. "The Politics of Metaphor." MLA Convention. New York City, 27 December 1986.

Ede, Lisa, and Andrea Lunsford. "Audience Addressed/Audience Invoked: The Role of Audience in Composition Theory and Pedagogy." *College Composition and Communication* 35 (1984): 155–71.

Faigley, Lester and Kristine Hansen. "Learning to Write in the Social Sciences." *College Composition and Communication* 36 (1985): 140–49.

Farrell, Thomas B. "Aspects of Coherence in Conversation and Rhetoric." *Conversational Coherence: Form, Structure, Strategy,* ed. Robert T. Craig and Karen Tracy, 259–84. Beverly Hills: Sage Publications, 1983.

———. "Knowledge, Consensus, and Rhetorical Theory." *Quarterly Journal of Speech* 62 (1976): 1–14.

Fish, Stanley. "Consequences." *Against Theory: Literary Studies and the New Pragmatism,* ed. W. J. T. Mitchell, 106–31. Chicago: University of Chicago Press, 1985.

———. *Is There a Text in This Class?: The Authority of Interpretive Communities,* Cambridge: Harvard University Press, 1980.

———. *Self-Consuming Artifacts: The Experience of Seventeenth-Century Literature.* Berkeley: University of California Press, 1972.

Fisher, Walter R. "Narration as a Human Communication Paradigm: The Case of Public Moral Argument." *Communication Monographs* 51 (1984): 1–22.

Flower, Elizabeth, and Murray G. Murphey. *A History of Philosophy in America.* New York: G. P. Putnam's Sons, 1977.

Foss, Sonya K., Karen A. Foss, and Robert Trapp. *Contemporary Perspectives on Rhetoric.* Prospect Heights, Ill.: Waveland Press, 1985.

Freed, Richard C., and Glenn J. Broadhead. "Discourse Communities, Sacred Texts, and Institutional Norms." *College Composition and Communication* 38 (1987): 154–65.

Frentz, Thomas S. "Rhetorical Conversation, Time, and Moral Action." *Quarterly Journal of Speech* 71 (1985): 1–18.

Friedman, Maurice S. *Martin Buber: The Life of Dialogue.* Chicago: University of Chicago Press, 1960.

Gadamer, Hans George. *Truth and Method.* New York: Seabury, 1975.

Gage, John T. "An Adequate Epistemology for Composition: Classical and Modern Perspectives." *Essays on Classical Rhetoric and Modern Discourse,* ed. Robert J. Connors, Lisa S. Ede, and Andrea A. Lunsford, 152–69. Carbondale: Southern Illinois University Press, 1984.

Geertz, Clifford. *The Interpretation of Cultures: Selected Essays.* New York: Basic Books, 1973.

———. *Local Knowledge: Further Essays in Interpretive Anthropology.* New York: Basic Books, 1983.

Goodrich, Chauncey Allen. *Select British Eloquence* (1852). Intro. Bower Ely. New York: Bobbs-Merrill, 1963.

Graff, Gerald. *Professing Literature: An Institutional History.* Chicago: University of Chicago Press, 1987.

Grice, H. P. "Logic and Conversation." *The Logic of Grammar,* ed. Donald Davidson and Gilbert Harman, 64–75. Encino, Calif: Dickenson Publishing Company, 1975.

Grimaldi, William M. A. *Studies in the Philosophy of Aristotle's Rhetoric.* Wiesbaden: Franz Steiner Verlag GmbH, 1972.

Halloran, S. Michael. "Letter From Camp." *The Sage Newsletter,* School of Humanities and Social Sciences, Rensselaer Polytechnic Institute. Fall 1987.

———. "Rhetoric in the American College Curriculum: The Decline of Public Discourse." *PRE/TEXT* 3 (1982): 245–69.

Hart, Roderick P., and Don M. Burks. "Rhetorical Sensitivity and Social Interaction." *Speech Monographs* 39 (1971): 75–91.

Heidegger, Martin. *Existence and Being.* Chicago: Henry Regnery Co., 1949.

Johannesen, Richard L. "The Emerging Concept of Communication as Dialogue." *Quarterly Journal of Speech* 57 (1971): 373–82.

Kennedy, George A. *Classical Rhetoric and Its Christian and Secular Tradition from Ancient to Modern Times.* Chapel Hill: University of North Carolina Press, 1980.

Kreckel, Marga. *Communicative Acts and Shared Knowledge in Natural Discourse.* London: Academic Press, 1981.

Kuhn, Thomas S. *The Structure of Scientific Revolutions,* 2d ed, enlarged. Chicago: University of Chicago Press, 1970.

LeFevre, Karen Burke. *Invention as a Social Act.* Carbondale: Southern Illinois University Press, 1987.

MacIntyre, Alisdair. *After Virtue: A Study in Moral Theory,* 2d ed. Notre Dame: University of Notre Dame Press, 1984.

McKeon, Richard. "Greek Dialectics: Dialectic and Rhetoric, Rhetoric and Dialogue." *Dialectics,* ed. Chaim Perelman, 1–25. The Hague: Martinus Nihjoff, 1975.

McLaughlin, Margaret. *Conversation: How Talk Is Organized.* Beverly Hills: Sage Publications, 1984.

Maimon, Elaine. "Talking to Strangers." *College Composition and Communication* 30 (1979): 364–69.

Miller, Carolyn R. "Genre as Social Action." *Quarterly Journal of Speech* 70 (1984): 151–67.

Myers, Greg. "Reality, Consensus and Reform in the Rhetoric of Composition Teaching." *College English* 48 (1986): 154–74.

Neel, Jasper. *Plato, Derrida, and Writing.* Carbondale: Southern Illinois University Press, 1988.

Oakeshott, Michael. "The Voice of Poetry and the 'Conversation of Mankind.'" *Rationalism In Politics*, 196–247. New York: Basic Books, 1962.

Ong, Walter J. *Orality and Literacy: The Technologizing of the Word.* London: Methuen, 1982.

———. "The Writer's Audience is Always a Fiction." *PMLA* 90 (1975): 9–21.

Orr, C. Jack. "How Shall We Say: 'Reality is Socially Constructed through Communication?'" *Central States Speech Journal* 29 (1978): 263–74.

Patton, John H. "Causation and Creativity in Rhetorical Situations: Distinctions and Implications." *Quarterly Journal of Speech* 65 (1979): 36–55.

Perelman, Chaim. "Authority, Ideology, and Violence." *The New Rhetoric and the Humanities: Essays on Rhetoric and its Applications*, 139–45. Dordrecht, Holland: D. Reidel Publishing Co., 1979.

———. "The Dialectical Method and the Part Played by the Interlocutor in Dialogue." *The Idea of Justice and the Problem of Argument.* Trans. John Petrie, 161–67. New York: Humanities Press, 1963.

———. "The New Rhetoric: A Theory of Practical Reasoning." *The New Rhetoric and the Humanities: Essays on Rhetoric and Its Applications*, 1–42. Dordrecht, Holland: D. Reidel Publishing Company, 1979.

———. "The Philosophy of Pluralism and the New Rhetoric." *The New Rhetoric and the Humanities: Essays on Rhetoric and Its Applications*, 62–72. Dordrecht, Holland: D. Reidel Publishing Co., 1979.

———. *The Realm of Rhetoric.* Trans. William Kluback. Notre Dame, Ind.: University of Notre Dame Press, 1982.

Perelman, Chaim, and M. Olbrechts-Tyteca. *The New Rhetoric: A Treatise on Argumentation.* Trans. John Wilkinson and Purcell Weaver. Notre Dame, Ind.: University of Notre Dame Press, 1969.

Plato. *Phaedrus.* Trans. W. C. Helmbold and W. G. Rabinowitz. Indianapolis: Bobbs-Merrill, 1956.

Rich, Adrienne. "The Cartographies of Silence." *The Dream of a Common Language: Poems 1974–1977.* New York: W. W. Norton, 1978.

Rorty, Richard. *Philosophy and the Mirror of Nature.* Princeton: Princeton University Press, 1979.

———. "Philosophy in America Today." *The American Scholar* (1981): 183–200.

Rosenfield, Lawrence W. "The Practical Celebration of the Epideictic." *Rhetoric in Transition: Studies in the Nature and Uses of Rhetoric*, ed. Eugene E. White, 131–55. University Park: Pennsylvania State University Press, 1980.

Royce, Josiah. "The Will to Interpret." *The Problem of Christianity*, 297–319. Chicago: University of Chicago Press, 1968.

Scott, Robert L. "Intentionality in the Rhetorical Process." *Rhetoric in Transition: Studies in the Nature and Uses of Rhetoric*, ed. Eugene E. White, 39–60. University Park: Pennsylvania State University Press, 1980.

Stewart, John. "Foundations of Dialogic Communication." *Quarterly Journal of Speech* 64 (1978): 183–201.

Todorov, Tzvetan. *Mikhail Bakhtin: The Dialogical Principle*. Trans. Wlad Godzich. Minneapolis: University of Minnesota Press, 1984.

Weaver, Richard. "Language Is Sermonic." *Contemporary Theories of Rhetoric: Selected Readings*, ed. Richard L. Johannesen, 163–79. New York: Harper and Row, 1971.

———. "The *Phaedrus* and the Nature of Rhetoric." *The Ethics of Rhetoric*, 1–26. Chicago: Henry Regnery Co., 1953.

White, Eugene E. "Rhetoric as Historical Configuration." *Rhetoric in Transition: Studies in the Nature and Uses of Rhetoric*, ed. Eugene E. White, 7–20. University Park: Pennsylvania State University Press, 1980.

Gregory Clark received his Ph.D. in 1985 from Rensselaer Poly-technic Institute. As Assistant Professor of English at Brigham Young University, he teaches rhetoric, writing, and early American literature. His current research examines the literature and public discourse of early America from a rhetorical perspective.